BORN PRIMITIVE
in the
Philippines

Bag-etan, 1954-

By Severino N. Luna

Edited with a Foreword
by Irene Murphy

SOUTHERN ILLINOIS
UNIVERSITY PRESS
Carbondale and Edwardsville

Feffer & Simons, Inc.
London and Amsterdam

CS11?

Library of Congress Cataloging in Publication Data

Luna, Severino N
  Born primitive in the Philippines.

  1. Bag-etan, 1954–   2. Mangyans. I. Title.
DS666.M3L86   959.9'3'040924[B]   75-23290

Contents

List of Illustrations

Foreword

The Filipino author of this book is Severino N. Luna, whom I call Benny. He has inexhaustible energy and insatiable curiosity. He lays his hand to many chores in behalf of his fellow citizens in the Philippines, and, whether he acts as amateur or professional, they seem to come off well. He has been a major in the resistance army, a businessman, an organizer of citizen movements in social welfare, and an administrator. He has now finished a book of popular anthropology.

We have been colleagues and family friends over a span of three decades, both in the Philippines and the United States. Professionally I am a social worker, teacher, educator, and activist in many social causes.

My first career in the Philippines was as a member of my brother-in-law's diplomatic family. He was the late Frank Murphy, the last American Governor General of the Islands.

Twelve years later, following World War II, I returned to the Philippines as director of an emergency program to render first-aid medical and social relief. We converted the million-dollar budget into jeeps, food supplies, medicines, and we spread out in teams over the 1,000-mile-long island nation by car and plane.

As the war ended, the rat population swelled enormously from the banquet of protein found in the fallen bodies of Japanese soldiers abandoned in the mountains. The rats multiplied, grew fat, tall, and strong enough to stand on their back legs and reap a whole rice clearing in a single night. The mountain people grew thin and starved. Because of the rats, Benny, then assigned as a rat exterminator, explored in Mindoro among the Mangyans and found the people he now writes about, while I spent an unforgettable week in Northern Luzon among the Bontoc-Igorots.

Hearing that there was actual starvation among the groups in the Luzon mountains, I organized a special rescue team. We had to take rat poison as an odd kind of relief. This was a touchy situation because we did not want it to get into the hands of warring tribes. We were three: a Belgian missionary priest in white soutane, who spoke the various dialects we would encounter, an Igorot jeep-driver in cast-off GI khaki, and myself. We had a two-wheel cargo trailer filled with our supplies. As we left Baguio we were warned not to go. The week before, the bones of two American anthropologists, long missing, had been found, their bodies mutilated and scattered over the barren rice fields in fertility rites. Fr. Louis Brasseur said they must have violated some local taboos. We spent a week on the perilous, zigzag, cliff-hanging mountain roads, driving through the night if we had not reached our destination. We soon heard what had happened to the anthropologists. They had cut across the territorial lines back from the roads. They had avoided identification or explanation of their invasion of territory, proof that they were hostile and dangerous. Warning signals were pounded out from village to village. They were finally sighted and killed for their bad manners.

During the trip through the Bontoc-Igorot area, as far as Sagada, I noticed Fr. Brasseur's punctilious etiquette. If our headlights showed up a single file of warriors with spears, on the road, we would stop immediately. So would they. The priest would identify us, as well as our purpose in being there. We would uncover the trailer and offer them our food. They accepted only matches. They, in turn, explained that they were taking their few family pots and pans to the lowland to barter or sell for food. They would not accept ours, saying we would need it ourselves.

Late one night, we approached an Igorot settlement where many ground fires still glowed. Fr. Brasseur, as usual, asked to be taken to the chief; again, the introductions and explanations. We were invited to join in the funeral feast of a man who had died of starvation. But he could not be buried until the last of his fowl and small animals had been roasted over a pit and eaten. Their laws of inheritance require that the next generation must start out with only the bare land and hand tools. The deceased was strapped into a rope seat and his body swung slowly high above the embers of the fire pit. We felt welcomed as we shared the food. The body, well smoked by then, would be buried when the food was gone.

Within a year after my return to the United States, a call from the United Nations asked me to accept a mission to the Philippines to open the first UN office in Manila and serve as a Social Affairs Officer. My job, working directly under President Manuel Roxas, was to help reactivate the dismantled social services or help create new ones. This was when I met Benny.

He had lived through the agony and chaos of the last days of the war and had become obsessed with the desire to organize a voluntary citizen's movement to save the social services. He had heard of the Community Chest movement in America and thought I might help him. It was easy. Under the auspices of the United Nations he received a travel grant to study the Community Chest organizations in the United States, in which I, too, had had experience. When he returned sixty days later, we went to work and within a few months, in 1949, held the first Community Chest campaign in Asia. It was a success, survived, and has continued to grow.

Other assignments followed, and I was asked to switch from social welfare to economic development in the rural areas. Under a joint UN-U.S. AID project, I became a Rural Industries Specialist, and was allowed to recruit a team of designers from Cranbrook Academy of Art, in Michigan, to help rural artisans redesign their handicraft products for export. Soon a pyramid of our new products touched off a design explosion that has led to a continued huge export of hand-manufactured goods to the American market. I decided to be a part of it. When I returned to the United States in 1954, I gave up my profession and became a designer-importer-wholesaler.

Incidentally, that was the year that Bag-etan, the chief character of this book, was born. By 1968, Benny met him at age fourteen at Siangi. Also, by that time I had been elected Regent of the University of Michigan and was involved in the many student-protest movements in the turbulent '60s when

This letter was written by Bag-etan in his inscriptional language to Irene Murphy and her assistants. The Mangyans are the only group in the Philippines that has preserved a written language. It is possibly three thousand years old and is classified as being Indic. The language is thought to have come from India, and before that possibly from the Mediterranean. The writing is in a phonetic code of characters. Severino Luna has made the following translation.

"Daddy Major has told me that you are helping him very much in getting the book of my life printed for the American people. I am very grateful to you. I want to tell you that what is written in the book about me is very true, nothing is false. Did Daddy Major tell you that it took him about three years to write the book and that he often worked up to past midnight? I know it because he always called me to his side when he wanted to ask me questions, whether we were in Manila or Siangi. I am happy and grateful to you for helping Daddy Major get the book printed."

Signed by the person of Bag-etan.   September 2, 1972

the life styles of our American youth changed so radically. When Benny sent me this three-volume, 300,000-word manuscript in 1972 I was impressed with this additional proof of his doggedness. Although he is a layman in the field of anthropology, his is a vivid personalized account of the day-by-day life and conversations with this group of primitive people. I advised him that the manuscript would have to be drastically shortened to gain a popular audience. He agreed and gave me full power of attorney to effect an abridgment.

That called for editorial help. By a set of uncanny coincidences two volunteers appeared: James G. Carey, a writer, and Pamela Gilson Laird, an editorial assistant. Both had lived in Asia and were intensely interested. We became a team of three and worked rapidly and in full accord with each other for ten months. The final abridgment is only about one-tenth the length of the original Luna manuscript. We shortened it in two ways. The Luna original had been a mixture of his own observations plus long dialogues with Bag-etan on a question-and-answer basis. Carey, the writer whom I call Jim, kept only the answers as given by Bag-etan, and sharpened them into an autobiography. Secondly, he selected only the episodes of Bag-etan's life story, which also revealed as much anthropological material as possible. In other words, only one or two funerals instead of dozens. Jim's job was a monumental one of rebuilding to retain substance and achieve brevity. Pamela then took Jim's 90,000-word manuscript and, by simple deletions, reduced it again so as to leave a simple, rather stark story which Bag-etan's limited vocabulary might have produced. Nothing was ever added, either of substance or style. We only sifted, then sifted again.

I wrote the section titles and enjoyed doing it, recalling my involvement with students at the Ann Arbor campus during the late '60s. This involvement with the Philippines has been as fascinating as all the preceding ones.

I give my profound thanks to Jim Carey and Pamela Gilson Laird for so greatly helping to make this edition of the book possible.

Birmingham, Michigan   Irene Murphy
February 27, 1975

Preface

This book is about the life, adventures, and romance of Bag-etan, a Mangyan Buhid teen-ager in the Philippines. A few days after he was born his mother died. As is the practice of Bag-etan's people he should have been buried alive, rather than be doomed to starve. He was saved, however, by his own mother who, before she died, extracted a promise from the father to find a nursing woman, which the father did and thus saved his life. Other than human milk the only food would be root crops or meat.

At about age ten he was snatched from the bedside of his dying father and was virtually enslaved by a cruel cowhand. He made a spectacular escape a year later and eventually found a new home in a distant Mangyan Buhid settlement. He then took his first child-wife. During the next four years he had many teen-age wives in succession, all in accordance with the custom of his people.

The Mangyan Buhids live in the mountain ranges of Mindoro where they try to shut out the creeping influences of civilization. Some anthropologists believe that they are a stranded remnant of an ancient people whose origins in Southeast Asia may go back three thousand years. The Mangyans are found exclusively on the island of Mindoro. They are not known to be warlike either among themselves or against non-Mangyans.

Mindoro island, the setting of this story, is a large area southwest of Luzon island. It is believed to be the Ma-i mentioned in Chinese chronicles as early as A.D. 900. It was believed to be a distribution center of Chinese merchants, where chiefs of various nearby islands came to barter.

Bongabon is the nearest town to the Mangyan Buhids in this story. It is a seaport and could have been used by Chinese traders hundreds of years ago. Siangi, where most of the action of this story took place, is a small sitio of Lisap, a barrio in Bongabon, and located on mountain ranges some 28 kilometers from the town proper.

From my studies and observations of this cultural minority, I would say that there are at least three distinct groupings, based on their social and economic life and cultural practices. These divisions to which the Buhids of Siangi frequently refer are:

The Patags, Mangyans who have come from their mountain homes, settled down with the lowlanders, whom they refer to as Logtanons, absorbed the lowlanders' economic life, culture, and dress. The Patags in fact live like the lowlanders.

The Buhids, who live in mountain ranges, cut the forests and burn the cut trees to plant a little rice, corn, casaba, bananas, and gabi, the basic foods they raise in the burned areas. They move from one burned forest to another. They run away from strange people who happen to pass by or wander into their surroundings, although once in a while they visit the town to buy their bolos, axes, salt, matches, and a few essentials they cannot produce themselves.

The Buhids of Siangi, the people in this story, grow their own cotton from which they make their thread and weave the G-string of their men and the abul and baruka of their women. Buhids from other areas of Mindoro do not know how to weave; neither do they grow cotton.

The Bangons live mostly by hunting and fishing and by raising root crops. Except for scant bark-cloth worn around the groin, the men and women are usually naked in their natural habitat. They have no known agricultural technology or tools. They never mix with people other than their own and they avoid any contact even with the Buhids, and run away or hide from the Patags. Likewise, the Buhids avoid them and generally look down on them, although there have been a few cases of intermarriage between the Buhids and Bangons. Bag-etan's grandfather was half Bangon and half Buhid of the Beribi tribe.

The Mangyans have their own indigenous system of writing which sets them apart from any other mountain people of the Philippines. How they developed it is the subject of much conjecture by anthropologists. I have shown some ancient Phoenician writing to Bag-etan. Strangely, he could sound it out because of the resemblance of the characters to the Mangyan, but he could not understand its meaning.

There is a high mortality rate among the Siangi Buhids, especially the infants. In spite of the cool weather generally prevailing throughout the year, children are naked from the time their mothers, alone in the bush, deliver them, until they are five to seven years old. Their diet consists mostly of root crops, fish from creeks, wild pigs, chicken, and deer from the forest.

The Siangi Buhids have their own unique system of government and laws as the reader will learn from this book.

My interest in the Mangyans was sharpened by a German priest we knew as Father Thiel, whom I first met in 1955. On the occasion when he said mass during a fiesta at Barrio Luna, a barrio named after me, he implored me to use my influence as Executive Director of the Philippine Rural Community Improvement Society (PRUCIS) to get the government to declare officially some one thousand hectares of logged-over forest in Bongabon as a Mangyan reservation so that the Mangyans could prevent "Christians from invading their land." Fortunately, a sympathetic Agriculture Secretary, Salvador Araneta, gave due process to my request and an equally sympathetic successor, Juan de G. Rodriguez, finally approved it; thus was established in Batangan, Bongabon, the first Mangyan reservation in Mindoro.

Ironically, having done so much to "keep the Christians out," I was the first one who wanted to be "in," but only as a friend. In 1963, I obtained a pastureland lease in Siangi, on the periphery of the area occupied by Buhids, whom I had rarely seen in town. Unlike the Patag Mangyans, my new neighbors are an extremely primitive group who prefer to live in the protective isolation of the forests. At first they would run and hide if they saw me or any stranger. It took my family several years to win their friendship. By bringing clothing, soap, matches, sugar, salt, and candies for their children, we convinced them of our sincere friendship. We were finally accepted as friends by a few, the first being Agaw—the Mangyan Chief in the story—and his children, to whom he wanted to give my family name as their family name, the Mangyans having no such names of their own.

I was also accepted by the adopted son of Agaw's family, Bag-etan of this story. He was about fourteen years old when I first met him in 1968. Bag-etan, having lost his own father at ten, has given me all of the loving trustfulness that a son would have for a father. He calls me "Daddy Major" because I was an officer in the resistance army, 1945–46.

My five years of close intimacy with Bag-etan and with his people provided me with the rare wealth of experiences and observations which I now share with you in *Born Primitive in the Philippines*. Bag-etan and I live and move together, both on my pastureland by the Siangi River which traverses the setting of this story and at our home in Quezon City, the capital of the Philippines. In both places at night, by oil light in the forest and fluorescent lamps in Quezon City, Bag-etan comes to my room and tells me of his life, loves, his adventures, his sorrows, his joys, and his hopes. We communicate through what I have learned of his language and what he has learned of Filipino. The friendship which has developed since then, and the gentle wisdom of Agaw that comes from the folklore of his people and from his experiences, and Bag-etan's own story of his extraordinary and exciting life, as well as my exhaustive research on the life and culture of the Mangyans, inspired me to write this book.

I sent the three-volume manuscript of three hundred thousand words to a dear friend and colleague in America, Irene Murphy, Birmingham, Michigan, requesting a reader's comment. She thought it was too long, hence too expensive for any publisher to take a risk.

Desiring American readership, I authorized Irene Murphy to edit and abridge the work to suit American readership and publishing standards, reserving, however, my right to publish the unabridged edition later.

I acknowledge here with deepest appreciation the unique contribution of a number of art students of the Philippine Women's University in Manila, under Director Mariano Madarang and his wife, for soliciting contributions of old clothes and cash to buy matches, salt, and soap for distribution to the Buhids in order to help win their friendship. To Dr. Constacio

Carpio and his wife for bringing medicine and ministering to the sick Buhids; to Mr. and Mrs. Esteban Magannon, who reviewed the original manuscript and made valuable suggestions to suit anthropological standards; to Severino Luna, Jr. and his wife Dr. Linda Luna, and Severino Luna, III, for their patience in teaching Bag-etan to read and write Filipino, which helped me immeasurably and solved our communication problem; to Irene Murphy and her editorial staff, James G. Carey and Pamela Gilson Laird, who produced this abridged edition of my original, and finally to my wife, who patiently bore with me the countless sleepless nights working on the manuscript, I express my gratitude.

Severino N. Luna

Manila, Philippines
December 24, 1974

Born Primitive in the Philippines

1 Enslaved and Orphaned

My happy childhood ended suddenly one day. It was the day that Mang José, a Logtanon—a person not of our valley—happened to visit our hut while hunting. He was carrying his badil and was followed by his dog. I was about ten years old. My memory of the events of that day never loses its vividness.

We lived in a river valley at the foothills of a mountain range in the eastern part of Mindoro. My father and I lived alone. My mother had died when I was born.

Mang José was the caretaker of a pasturage near our home. His barbarous appearance, made more so by the ominous badil he always carried and the stories of his savage cruelties, kept me fearful of him. I call him *Mang*, out of habit, to indicate respect for an older person.

Observing that my father, who was lying on his mat, made no attempt to get up, Mang José asked if he was seriously ill. My father explained that he was having severe coughing spells which made him spit blood. Mang José urged my father to walk to town and see a doctor as soon as possible.

At that point, Mang José noticed me and said, "Don't worry about your son, Tipig. I will take him with me and care for him until you get well. He can help me in the pastureland, and when I get my share, I'll give him a share too."

My father rejected Mang José's offer, explaining that the sickness would leave him as it always had in the past. But Mang José persisted in urging my father to see the doctor, even to the point of intimidating him by waving his badil in front of my father's face as he repeated the words, "Something might happen to you, Tipig."

1

My father finally relented and agreed that I would go with Mang José, but insisted that I must be returned as soon as he recovered. My father's words of consent, allowing me to be taken from home, made me cry unendingly. Unable to conceal my abhorrence of Mang José, I embraced my father and cried out, "I do not want to go with him! I am afraid of him!"

"Be brave, my son. It will be only for a short while," he said. "Then we'll be together again."

Before leaving the house, Mang José promised my father that he would send his brother to inform my sisters, Mabanay and Tomay, of our father's condition. This promise was made as Mang José dragged me out of the door. On the fantao I twisted my arm free from his grip and ran back into the house to kiss my father. Embracing me firmly, my father whispered, "Son, if he does not let you come back to me after I get well, escape and come to me. I love you and I need you."

Although I was sobbing as I kissed my father again, Mang José grabbed my hand and roughly yanked me away. Looking back, I could see the tears on my father's face, but I could not break free.

I cried all the way to Mang José's house. My father's last words to me, "Escape and come to me. I love you and need you," kept ringing in my head. I was tormented by disquieting questions: why did my father consider it necessary to tell me that? Did he suspect that Mang José might try to keep me forever?

When we were a long distance from my father's house, Mang José ordered me to walk in front of him with the warning that if I tried to run off he would shoot me. I was too terrorized to disobey him.

My first day with Mang José was humiliating. I was treated like a slave. I was forbidden to talk to anyone outside his household; I was not permitted to leave his pasturage; I could not allow anyone to come in to talk to me. He constantly threatened to shoot me if I attempted escape. That night I cried myself to sleep.

There were two other boys who were being kept in bondage by Mang José. Olando, a Logtanon, was about fourteen years old, and the other boy, Yagay, was, like me, a Buhid. He was only eight years old.

2

Our people are divided into three groups: the Buhids, the Patags, and the Bangons. There is another group known as the Beribi, but they are really an offshoot of the Buhids. The Buhids prefer to live in the mountains, and they engage in some trade with the Logtanons; the Patags have migrated to the lowlands and have intermarried with Logtanons there; but the Bangons remain the most isolated in the high mountain area.

The very faraway Logtanons, whom we call Filipinos or Tagalogs, call all of us Mangyans. They don't understand our separate group names. We use our own names.

Although my mother was part Bangon, I was born in Yamyamo, which is a Beribi settlement. Later we moved to Mayoma, which is populated by Buhids. I grew up as a Buhid.

For three weeks, Mang José was perpetually irritated by my begging for information about my father and my requests to visit him. He threatened to beat me soundly if I continued to pester him.

Olando, Yagay, and I were required to help Mang José with his duties as overseer of the pasturage. We usually led the cows to pasture each morning and watched them throughout the day. The work was boring and completely wretched on those days when it rained or was extremely hot. In the afternoon we herded the cows back to a corral, and if any of the herd went astray, Mang José would beat us with a stick he kept just for that purpose. We were frequently beaten for the slightest infraction of his rules. Although he was brutally intolerant of any violations of his own rules, he did not respect the rules of others. He trained us to steal chickens, coconuts, and other crops from the surrounding plantations, and he beat us severely if we refused to do his thieving for him.

At the beginning of the eleventh month with Mang José I received a visit from Naay, my sister Tomay's husband. My delight was boundless, for I was sure he had come to free me. That moment of joy was quenched when Naay informed me that my father had been dead for two months.

When I was finally able to realize my father was dead I lost all fear of Mang José, who was standing nearby listening to our conversation. I denounced him as evil and vicious for not telling me of my father's death. My whole body trembled with

3

rage when Naay told me that someone had informed Mang José that my father was dying and had repeatedly asked to see me.

As he left, Naay embraced me and reminded me of my father's last instructions to escape. Mang José would not allow me to leave with Naay, threatening that if I went he would accuse me of stealing.

I was overwhelmed with feelings of loneliness and loss. I kept remembering my father with tears on his face as I was torn from him by Mang José. I did not believe that I would ever recover from my grief.

Mang José shrewdly avoided me all that day. Olando offered me the only relief that could have eased my pain: he broached the subject of escape. My first reaction was that we should leave immediately, but he dismissed that as too rash. He assured me that he and Yagay would select the best opportunity for our successful escape.

A month passed but neither of the boys gave any indication of when we might leave. My confidence in Olando was diminishing when Mang José suddenly told us that he and his wife would be away for two days. We were warned that if we left the area we would be beaten upon his return, and if we escaped he pledged to track us down and shoot us.

Mang José and his wife were barely out of sight when Olando urged us to prepare for our escape. We would go to different destinations; Yagay was going to his father's place, and we were to travel partway together. I was going to Siangi in the eastern part of Mindoro.

First, Yagay and I accompanied Olando to the junction where the jeepney bus stopped. We all hid so we could watch for it without exposing ourselves to someone who might tell Mang José. A jeepney finally pulled up, but it was filled. People were sitting on the hood and others were clinging to the back. Olando found a handgrip there. As it started down the road he was holding fast with one hand and waving frantically to us with the other as distance gradually separated us from view.

There was no transportation to Siangi or to the place Yagay was headed; so we decided to return to Mang José's house to get food. We planned to start out early the next morning.

4

Arriving at Mang José's house we searched for food. There was none. Yagay then dug up some gabi while I searched for matches. I could not find a single one. We then walked quite a distance to the nearest neighbor, Agday, who kindly gave us saba which also had to be cooked. Agday then gave us lighted embers to start our fire.

A downpour started as we walked back from Agday's house, and it extinguished our embers. Our hopes of going inside Mang Jose's house were also quickly extinguished when we heard his familar roaring threats to his wife coming from the house and realized they had come home a day early.

Our bodies were soaked, we were shivering from the cold rain, and our spirits were chilled by the forboding words of Mang José. We decided to run back to Agady's hut, sure that he would help our escape.

Agday, evidently, had decided to go to his hut downstream, for he was not in his own where we found some camotes which we devoured raw. In the darkness we took off our G-strings and wrung them out to dry. We huddled together in a corner for warmth until we fell asleep.

There was only a hint of dawn when Yagay woke me to say he heard a dog barking. When I heard it I jumped up ready for flight. I was already on the fantao when I discovered my nakedness. "My G-string!" I exclaimed. Yagay could only laugh at my panic. Of course it was absurd to waste precious seconds retrieving my G-string. If Mang José had caught up with us he would have fulfilled his threat to shoot us. We ran until exhausted, then hid under a thick bush to rest. Lying there, we could no longer hear the dog barking. Working downstream we found Agday in his hut.

He agreed to help us. He thought our plan of separate directions was sound. He gave each of us some boiled bananas and camotes for the journey. We thanked Agday for all of his friendly help. I embraced Yagay with reassuring words, and we went our separate ways.

The Buhids I met while hiking confirmed the accuracy of Agday's directions to Siangi, which reassured me greatly, because Agday had mentioned that possibly I had relatives there.

One of the peculiarities of our people is the way we measure things. It is said that we measure distances by the number of hand-rolled tobacco-leaf cigarettes smoked in travel. Therefore, when I asked someone how far I was from a particular landmark, he would say that it was one or two cigarettes from where we were standing. With little else to occupy my mind, I tried measuring distances in this manner with some crudely rolled leaves. I was amazed at the accuracy. But smoking tobacco is secondary to us. We prefer to chew it, which is another unique means for measuring distance. The Buhid term *embasan mama* means the chewing of tobacco, betel-nuts, or betel-leaves. It is estimated to take one hour from the moment the mixture is put into the mouth, chewed until it is tasteless, and thrown away. The word *duak* means two, so duak embasan mama means "two chewings" or two hours.

The sun is our clock. A common question asked when entering a Buhid house is, "Where was the sun when you arrived?" to determine the time of day. The Buhid expression *mianit mashohod mita* is the time when the sun hits your eyes at a forty-five-degree angle, which is 10:00 A.M. by a Logtanon clock. A rokiawan is the farthest distance a strong shout can carry and still be audible.

It was mianit kalimbaba—3:00 P.M.—when I saw a Buhid hut. I asked the old man and his wife who lived there if I could sleep on their fantao. They engaged me in the typical conversation to find out the story of my life before they consented. Explaining why I was going to Siangi, I revealed my ordeal with Mang José. There were tears in their eyes as I finished. Instead of offering me their fantao, they insisted that I sleep inside with them. In fact, they suggested I stay with them permanently. I was overwhelmed with their generosity, but I was even more filled with fear when I realized how near they were to Mang José. I explained the reason why I could not stay with them. The old lady woke me early the next morning. A breakfast of camotes was already prepared, plus some potatos for me to take with me. She helped pack them away in my bayong, an indispensable part of a Buhid's gear.

Long after leaving the hut, still engrossed in unscrambling the various landmarks I was to watch for, I was suddenly shocked at realizing I had not asked the names of the couple.

About bok sirang—12:00—I came upon a creek I had been

told to watch for. It meant I was near Siangi. I was excited and happily relieved. I jumped in to take a much needed bath in celebration. Refreshed but hungry, I ate the last of the camotes and lay down for a brief nap.

I was awakened by a Logtanon who thought I might have been injured and was unconscious. I learned from him that I was already in Siangi. Following the creek downstream, I spotted a Buhid house perched on a hill. Since it was sunset, I approached to ask if I might sleep on the fantao that night.

My weary appearance must have caused the man to invite me inside. After answering several questions about myself I learned that the man was my mother's cousin. His name was Malanoy and his wife's name was Lukdo. He knew my father, and was saddened when I told of his death.

Such a cordial reception after the abuses I had endured and the discovery that I had found relatives brought tears of joy. During the evening meal, Malanoy told me the story of my infancy. My mother died a few days after my birth. Under such circumstances it is the Buhid custom to bury the infant alive with the mother in a common grave. Otherwise, the infant will be doomed to starve from lack of human milk. I have since learned that infants can be fed with the milk of animals, but at the time of my mother's death this was not known by her people.

Malanoy told me that my father had promised his beloved wife that he would not bury me alive. But he was in a great dilemma. I was his only male offspring. He was sure that I would starve. How could he carry out his promise to his dead wife?

I was spared this premature death, whether by burial alive or starving, by a fortunate coincidence. A relative of ours with the same name as my sister, Tomay, had recently given birth to a male and agreed to nurse me also.

This narrative of my mother's death and of my miraculous escape from death caused me to cry like an infant.

The love shown to me by Malanoy and Lukdo compared to the brutality I had been living through with Mang José made me determined to never let him find me. I thought of an idea and discussed it with these two kind people. Why not change my name so Mang José could not trace me? He knew me by my birth name, which was Bay-in. I would give myself a new name. I chose Bag-etan. When I suggested this name to Malanoy and Lukdo, she giggled because it means "one who starts a fire with friction." But they agreed and we all laughed at my new identity.

They treated me as a son. In spite of their poverty and with two small children to feed, they tried to hide the strain I put on their food supply.

A couple of weeks after my arrival, Agaw, the Chief of the Buhids in Siangi, visited them. He was widely loved and respected as being a wise, kind leader. Like all Buhids, Chief Agaw was very short and sinewy. Although his hair was turning gray, his face was unwrinkled. He had a deep, warm laugh. His face revealed his moods. A gentle expression indicated relaxation; a stern face meant he was trying to solve a problem.

To my utter surprise, when Malanoy explained my situation to Chief Agaw, he invited me to come and live with his family. I was so stunned at this honor that I could not respond. He noticed my awkwardness. Then I learned an important moral lesson from him. He told me to express myself frankly even though I might offend him. "Remember always, Bag-etan," he said, "do not ever be afraid to tell the truth, because truth is strength."

I finally blundered out how honored I felt and accepted the offer. Both men kept referring to some "beautiful bags" that Agaw had, and assured me that I would be given one when I went to live with him. I did not understand this remark.

The sadness at parting with Malanoy and his family was mutual, but we all realized that survival for all dictated this decision.

Befitting his position, Chief Agaw's house was bigger than the others. It was about two cigarettes from Malanoy's house, a two-hour hike.

Agaw's wife, Yonay, was as tall as her hushand; she seemed to smile perpetually even though her lips did not part—her whole face smiled. Her natural charm made her seem youthful.

Being introduced to their five sons, I noticed that Agaw raised his voice to the one named Lando. Another, Rahoyan, was obviously a very sensitive boy. Of their three daughters,

8

Agaw, chief of the Buhids in the Siangi River area and Bag-etan's foster-father.

All photographs, unless otherwise specified, are by Severino N. Luna.

Amit, who was about my age, caught my attention. She was slightly plump. Her easy smile and warm, glowing eyes attracted me. Concluding the introductions, Agaw addressed Amit, saying "Here's a nice dog for you. Take care of him so he'll grow fat." Unused to their ways, I was offended at being referred to as a dog. Later, I asked Agaw about the "beautiful bag" I had been promised. He seemed amused, and answered, "You will soon discover that you have already seen the bag."

As a member of the family, I joined the others in working on Agaw's kaingin. I planted and cared for the camotes, the

9

Chief Agaw and his wife, Yonay, at their home in Siangi, December 1970.

gabi, and a variety of other vegetables, which were new to me. The other boys delighted in teasing me about my size—I was less than four feet tall—and to prove myself I worked to the limit of my strength. I tried manfully to perform all of the chores of kaingin: clearing bushes, digging undergrowth, plowing soil.

Agaw's success in supporting a large family was because of his expert management. He would settle only for maximum efficiency. Some of us specialized just in the vegetables. Others cared for coffee and banana plants and coconut trees. This gave the family variety and abundance.

We Buhids strive for only two fundamentals: enough food and adequate shelter. In a G-string culture, clothing is unim-

Chief Agaw and his family on the fantao of their home, which is slightly larger but otherwise typical of the Mangyan huts. The roof is of cogon, the walls are of bark of trees, and the ladder is one long, sturdy branch of a tree.

portant. Families that have food and shelter are regarded as comfortable. Agaw's family was regarded as prosperous because they had abundant food, a large house, and clothing as they needed.

The food staples are camotes, gabi, rice, coconuts, and bananas. The extra luxuries are papayas, pineapples, and avocados. Nature provides us with animals for meat. The G-strings worn by males and the breast bands and waist panels worn by women are made from cotton we grow, which is spun and woven by our women. Every item used in building our houses comes from the forest: wood, palm leaves, and tough grasses. Instead of purchasing steel nails we use vines and wooden pegs. We burn a tree sap called sahing for light. We do, however, purchase axes, bolos, knives, matches, salt, and beads from the Logtanons, using the money they give us for our surplus crops.

Living with Agaw's family was very pleasant, especially be-

11

cause of the close attention shown to me by Amit. I gradually realized that Amit was the "beautiful bag" I had been promised by Agaw. It is customary for the Buhids to express lovemaking in metaphors. When a boy says he wants to "catch a bird" or "tie a dog," he literally means he is searching for a mate.

Amit showed affection for me and gave me hints by flirtation. I tried to ignore them because of my respect for Agaw. I thought he would disapprove. Finally, one night she came to my mat on the floor and lay beside me, caressing me. After we made love, she remained and slept beside me all night. The affair worried me because I thought Agaw would be angry, but the next day he let me know he was aware I had accepted his "beautiful bag." By Buhid custom we were considered to be married by the simple fact that everyone in the household accepted our new relationship. Agaw counseled us to make our marriage a success, although neither of us was yet thirteen years old.

Child marriages are common among the Buhids of Siangi. These children live together as husband and wife, although the parents attempt to conceal the fact from strangers. It is customary for the new husband to present a hinoyo—dowry—to the bride's father. Multicolored strings of beads are the accepted currency. Agaw waived the hinoyo knowing of my poverty.

It was decided that Amit and I would still live with Agaw, principally to preserve the secret of our marriage, but it was soon known to everyone in the Siangi area. Amit and I then set up our own kaingin at a site selected by Agaw. Two of Amit's brothers, Anagon and Lando, helped me clear the land and build a makeshift hut. With a generous supply of corn from Agaw, we planted our first crop. Agaw was equally generous with his praise of me, predicting I would be a good husband to his daughter and eventually a good chief of our people.

Only a few days after we became married we heard that Amit's brother, Baban, had not been home for several days. No one became alarmed because they assumed he had gone to the western part of Mindoro. But later Agaw remarked that it was unlike Baban to go on any long trip without telling him. A search of the surrounding area proved fruitless.

12

A few days later Talad came running to Agaw's house, screaming that she had found Baban's body in a hut next to their kaingin. Baban lay in a large circle of blood on the floor. His head had been brutally severed from the body and was left hanging from the rafters. Soneone had stupidly attempted to make it appear that Baban had hanged himself.

That gruesome tragedy left Agaw and Yonay stunned with grief. Of their five sons, Baban was the least likely to have an enemy. This opinion was shared by all who knew him. We had, therefore, no suspect until Baban's wife mentioned that a young man named Eg-hay had hinted he was interested in her while Baban was still living. Although she dismissed this as a motive, Eg-hay became the sole suspect.

We buried Baban near the hut, and as is Buhid custom we burned the hut in which he had been killed.

After Baban's burial, Agaw was rarely at home. He devoted himself exclusively to gleaning evidence against Eg-hay. About a month later, Lando told us Agaw had brought the matter to the attention of Yaum, who was like the mayor of the larger settlement, so that a formal confrontation could be arranged between Agaw and Eg-hay and a decision on the case could be made according to our laws. Although I never learned exactly what occurred at that confrontation, I did hear from Anagon that Eg-hay consented to pay Agaw one hundred pesos. Under our laws if the aggrieved party agrees to the settlement, as Agaw did, the case can never be reopened.

Amit and I were too young to be confidantes of Agaw; so we refrained from asking him for details. Baban's death had a deep effect on the whole family. Each sought solace in his own way. Agaw restlessly moved from place to place in the area because, Yonay said, at home he was constantly reminded of Baban. Amit and I became engrossed in working on our kaingin and making improvements on our crudely constructed home. We sold the surplus from our first harvest of corn to the Logtanons, but the money we received only permitted us to buy a few arms' lengths of panaongens.

Lando, who became a frequent visitor, taught me our language. The various forest people of Mindoro are called Mangyans, which includes all of them. They are the only group in the Philippines known to have their own system of writing. This employs rigid matchstick, angular characters set in slant-positions to each other. Some people say it goes back thousands of years.

I also learned Mangyan songs from Lando. With my new skill in writing the language I was able to inscribe the words of these songs on pieces of bamboo. I soon had a good collection. A number of boys my own age were friends of ours, and for a pastime we sang songs we had learned or improvised as we went along, to the delight of Lando. Often Anagon would come with Lando, but Anagon was so partial to the sad, plaintive songs that we had a hard time to get him to sing gay songs and laugh. Though Lando was hard-of-hearing he could compose tender, sentimental songs, each with an interesting story. I was closer to Lando and Anagon than to any of Amit's other brothers. For me, they were the brother companions I had always wanted.

These sessions led to our being invited into the Buhids' social life. We were invited to attend poncions. Poncions are feasts. One eats his fill, ceases only long enough to digest what he has consumed, then returns for more. A poncion lasts until the food is gone.

While the parents are preoccupied with such indulgences, the boys and girls sing and make love. A poncion is given to celebrate an important or happy occasion. It is a community occasion at which everyone is welcome.

The first poncion I attended was sponsored by two men who had been fined one pig each by Chief Agaw, for fighting. The two squealing pigs were butchered, and a poncion was ordered so the two offenders could make a public apology and a pledge not to fight again, in accordance with Agaw's orders. Agaw shrewdly exploited the conflict to promote future peace. He congratulated each offender for his manly admission of his fault, but warned him that future fines would increase with each offense. It was impressive to see those two fierce-looking men be so respectful of the tiny but wiry Chief. He was regarded by all as a judicious, venerable leader. I was proud to be a member of his family.

2 "Never hate . . . it will destroy you"

My attachment to Agaw and Yonay was so warm that I addressed Agaw as father and Yonay as mother. They demonstrated their appreciation of my attempts to make Amit a worthy husband.

Then Amit became apathetic toward me. In place of the keen excitement she used to show in my plans for our kaingin, she was now indifferent. I thought it might be a passing mood but it did not improve. It hardened into an estrangement. I finally concluded that some other man had distracted her, and very shortly I found the man.

When I used to find Oto, an older boy who frequented our hut, talking to Amit when I came home from working our kaingin, I did not think it significant. Then I reviewed our failing relationship and realized it had started to cool about the time Oto began to visit our hut. Several times Oto brought firewood with him and helped Amit with her chores. Most important, I saw the flattering way Amit treated Oto.

When I could tolerate the situation no longer, I asked her what Oto meant to her. I was dismayed when she replied she thought we should separate. She calmly explained that when she married me she expected the union to last only a few weeks. Now it had lasted over a year and she wanted to try another husband. Amit consoled me with a reminder that my status as her first husband would give me legal rights over her. Amit was referring to the Mangyan custom that gives the first husband the option of making love to a wife from whom he has parted. If she consents, her second husband cannot object. If a woman and her first husband decide to remarry, her current husband must separate from her.

In spite of this I was upset by the brusque way she told me her decision. It hurt like a wound from a jagged knife.

I resigned myself to the separation, but I was reluctant to tell Agaw and Yonay because of all they had suffered from Baban's death. However, they were sure to learn of it, so I decided to

15

report to them at the first opportunity. When I did, Agaw was deeply offended with Amit for not getting his permission before separating. It is the custom in child marriages that the couple do not separate without their parents' permission. Oto was annoyingly calm when I asked him his plans for moving in with Amit. He said he would pay me any number of panaongens as a fine, but I flatly refused to accept anything from him. Since Oto paid me no fine I was preserving my rights over Amit for the future.

I moved back into Agaw's house, and Oto moved away with Amit to Tauga, several miles upstream from Siangi. Amit made a point to kiss me before they left, but I could not watch them actually leave. Agaw, watching them depart, was saddened. Amit was only fourteen years old, but, by custom, she was compelled to go with her husband.

After that the days following were a void I could not fill. I had the conceited notion that Amit would tire of Oto and return to me, but after a month that delusion evaporated. I lost interest in everything that used to give me pleasure, even my kaingin.

Agaw did all he could to revive my spirits; he invited me to go hunting with him; he rounded up other children my age for company. I was so touched that I did everything I could to conceal my feelings.

One day, Paladan, an old friend of Agaw's, visited the house. He told the old Chief he had heard I had "caught one of Agaw's chickens, but it had flown away already." In confirming this, Agaw explained he still hoped the chicken would return to the roost so I could tie her down again.

Paladan suggested that I take part in the harvest on his kaingin. I readily accepted because it would take me away from the scene of my painful memories. Agaw urged me to come back in one week because he was sure my "chicken" would be back by then.

Paladan and I reached his house in time for the noon meal. We started to work in his kaingin a few hours later. Paladan tried to cheer me up with a prediction that some "nice birds might come our way." Magically, a short time later, a girl a few years younger than I passed by. She was so beautiful my spine tingled. Just as I was bundling some rice, a second girl as pretty as the first strolled past and gave me a tantalizing smile. All I could think about were those two beautiful girls. Then I wondered how I looked to them. My G-string was improvised: a piece of rag crudely held up by a vine, the mark of wretched poverty. I vowed I would sell my portion of the harvest to buy a presentable G-string in case I met either of those beautiful girls again. They must live somewhere near, I thought, because "chickens" cannot fly very far. I resumed my work with such gusto I didn't look up until Paladan shouted to me to stop.

I was amazed that it was already getting dark and my fellow harvesters, including the two girls, were watching me. Paladan helped me gather and carry the stalks I had picked to his house, where an estimator would determine their value so I could be paid. While we were walking back I told Paladan of my intentions to use my earnings to purchase a new G-string.

Paladan rightly guessed I had spotted the two "pretty birds." He told me they were the daughters of his neighbor, Entas. The younger was Banglad and the elder was Emian. Paladan insisted that he introduce me to their parents, Entas and Yawi. I followed Paladan haltingly, because I was painfully self-conscious about my ragged appearance. Entas and his gracious wife put me at ease right away. Both girls resembled their mother. Entas told me of their long friendship with Agaw and his family. They expressed their sorrow over Baban's death, making it apparent they wanted any further information I could give them. I did not mention Eg-hay because my own opinion of his guilt was so hazy.

Paladan told me he would ask one of the estimators if I could get some earnings right away so I could buy a new G-string. Returning from the estimator, Paladan told me I was still one peso short of the price of a G-string.

To my embarrassment, Entas loudly announced to all the harvesters that I wanted to buy a new G-string, but was one peso short. He asked them to donate that sum to my cause.

I reviewed this curious set of events. I recalled, in Paladan's conversation with Agaw, something being said about my prospects for "catching a nice chicken" at his harvest, and how he had predicted in his kaingin that some nice birds would come along. Obviously Entas's public appeal for the

17

peso for my G-string was staged. His eyes rested on his two daughters, who had become the focus of everyone's attention.

There was a long silence, unbearable to me. Emian finally broke that silence, "We cannot be so unkind as to neglect our visitor." With that sentiment, she contributed a portion of her harvest to me. She said, "I hope you get the nicest G-string ever woven," leaving me so befuddled I was only able to murmur, "Thank you."

The harvest lasted for three more days. It was apparent to all my fellow harvesters that no rooster was more determined to catch a chicken than I was, in my pursuit of Emian. A bit of artifice brought us together to finish the harvest. I fumbled through my proposal, but she made it appear she thought me eloquent, and she consented to marry me. I escorted her home to ask permission from her parents.

Entas was well aware of our desire. He and Yawi readily approved our marriage. Entas also waived the required dowry, a decision he insisted on announcing to the group that had returned from the harvest with Entas and Yawi.

The announcement brought shouts of approval. In compliance with their demands, Emian and I kissed vigorously. The Mangyans' style of kissing is to rub noses. The more vigorous the nose rubbing, the more passionate the kiss.

Embracing Emian, Yawi gave her a buri mat, while Entas presented me with a blanket. This ritual is symbolic of marriage. The mat symbolizes the woman's obligation to serve her husband, and the blanket the man's protection and authority toward his family. Because this ceremony was performed by the bride's parents, it signified their acceptance and approval of the marriage.

Entas declared an impromptu celebration for that same evening, ordering an impressive number of chickens and twenty-five pounds of rice. An impromptu poncion, especially in the evening, is a great compliment to the person honored.

We fled to the seclusion of Emian's hut long before the poncion ended. Emian was thirteen years old and I was one year older, but this was a second marriage for both of us. I was relieved to learn that Emian's first husband had accepted the prescribed fines when he separated from her, and so had no conjugal rights over her.

The third day, we began clearing away foliage for our own kaingin. Recognizing our youth, Entas took over the supervision of the careful, long process. The first step in preparing a kaingin is to cut the shrubs under the trees, a process the Buhids call *gamas*. About a week later, when the shrubs are fairly dry, the secondary trees (about waist-high) are cut and left to dry, an operation known as *gubang wan*. The large trees are then cut down, which is called *sayogubang sayong tipco*. Then the branches are cut into short lengths, and the cleared area is left to dry—gal hag—which takes between one or two months, depending on the size of the trees.

When the area is dry enough, the clearing is fired—manlabay—generally at night. This must be so timed that it is not done too soon before the rainy season. After the first burning, the unburned twigs are gathered and placed in the trunks of the larger trees for a second conflagration. If the timing is wrong, wild grass will fill in the area. If this is not attended to quickly, the area will have to be done again, or else crops will not grow.

Entas decided we should wait a week before we undertook the second step. I took advantage of this holiday to visit Tatay Agaw and tell him of my marriage. To find Agaw in bed at napnoan sa gamat—2:00 p.m.—was cause for alarm, especially since he was weakened by a severe cough. Greeting me, Agaw congratulated me on my marriage to Emian. Few events occurred in our settlement that Chief Agaw did not know of within an incredibly short time.

I was relieved when he asked me to go with Lando to visit a Logtanon called "the Major," who would give us medicine to cure his coughing. Lando told me that Agaw and many other Buhids referred to the Major as a blood brother—Sindogo—because of his countless kindnesses.

To please the Major, we washed in the creek before going into his house. Normally the Buhids wait several months between baths, but the Major's coaxing and the free soap induced us to wash oftener than this.

I experienced other unusual things at the Major's. I saw Buhid children who were afraid of Logtanons sit on his lap. I could not believe it when I saw Buhid women kiss the Major in the presence of their husbands and strangers. Lando finally

19

persuaded me to meet the Major. Before we left, he gave Lando medicine, salt, matches, and meat for Agaw.

On the trip back, Lando told me about the beautiful colored fire bombs the Major fires into the sky to signal his arrival to his Buhid friends. The following day the people who want to see him go to his house. From Lando I learned that his brother, Anagon, wanted to go to Manila with the Major, but the Major was going to talk to Agaw before he would agree to Anagon's request. The deep affection so many Buhids showed the Major so impressed me that I could appreciate Anagon's desire to see the marvelous sights of a city under his guidance. Because Anagon wished to go there, I also had the desire. But I was now happily married, so I dismissed the notion.

Sleep in Agaw's house that night was impossible. I kept remembering the many nights I had shared with Amit on the spot where I now lay alone in torment. Yonay, as usual, had a good breakfast waiting for us. When I later went to bid Agaw good-bye, there were a few things he wished to tell me.

"Bag-etan, I wish I had the power to hold you with us permanently," Agaw said between his coughing spells, "but you are growing into a young man and desire to face the world on your own. That is good. Here is a little advice. You are now married a second time. It is possible you'll be married another time because you are so young. Do not let your eyes be the only judge in selecting a wife. Your eyes can deceive you. You must observe and learn; there are many birds in the air. All of them are beautiful to look at, but not all of them are good. Even the snake in the grass is attractive, but you must beware: it can kill you.

"So, my son, remember, beauty is not always a good guide for picking a wife. And remember, also, when walking through a forest you will arrive where you are going faster, if you look back once in a while to see where you started.

"When you hear a noise, don't be like the wild pig that jumps and runs away only to fall into a trap. Stop, sit down, listen, look around, and then make your decision. Do not be so overly brave that you fear nothing. That is foolishness. Neither should you be cowardly. The man who is afraid of snakes will finally come upon one, panic, and be bitten by it. The man afraid of bees will never know the sweet taste of honey.

"Youth is the period of learning; manhood is the period of understanding and action; and old age is the period of explaining to the younger men. Do not attempt to do all these things at the same time. Live and act in accordance with your time period."

"Tatay," I said, "all the things you are telling me sound good, but I do not understand them very well."

"I know this," said Agaw. "You are still too young to understand what I'm trying to tell you, but do try to remember it. In time the earth, the water, the animals, the birds, and even tiny insects in the forest will teach you lessons better than I could do. Just be observant.

"Bag-etan, I have great hopes for you. Someday you'll become a leader of our people and take my place. I am sorry I cannot say the same thing about my other sons: Rahoyan is too timid. Lando has the qualities of a leader, but he cannot hear too well, and Anagon has no interest. You are my one hope. Someday, when you grow a little older, you must go with the Major to Manila and learn more. He can teach you many things, especially about the laws of the Logtanons, so you can lead our people wisely. You must learn to read the Logtanons' language so you can gain their knowledge. As you can see, I'm very ill and may not live long. If I die without a good leader to take my place, our people will be put under Yaum, the Mayor of the Batangans, who is trying to bring the Buhids in Siangi under the control of his deputy, Saguim. They impose fines on the people."

"I hate those two. They are enemies of our people!" was my reaction.

"Son," he said, a little impatience in his tone, "*hate* and *enemy* are two words you should never be quick to use until you have a full understanding of them. You should never hate anyone or consider anyone your enemy. It is better to have one friend and no enemies than to have many friends and a single enemy. Yaum and Saguim are not our enemies, nor do I hate them. I do not like the way they run things, but if I try to hate them and make them our enemies there would soon be two warring groups, and what would that bring? We would be so taken up with hating each other we would not be able to do anything else. The important things that go with maintaining life would be put aside so we could direct all our abilities toward destruction of each other. In the end we would all starve.

"When they do something you recognize as wrong, instead of hating them for their actions, try to learn from them. You know Baban did not commit suicide, as his murderer tried to make us believe; Baban was murdered, and I have every right to hate the man who did that to my son. But if I start hating, I might come to hate him enough to kill the man I suspect of murdering my son, his relatives would want to kill me. Now, where would the end be? Disaster for all of us."

The long talk recalling Baban's death started Agaw coughing severely, so I reminded him that it was almost noon and I had better start toward home. I embraced him firmly, and promised I would remember everything he had told me.

Lohena, the youngest daughter, was sitting on the fantao. "Good-bye Lohena," I said, patting her gently on the head. She held my hand tightly and would not let go. Our eyes met, and her message was clear. I tactfully turned my head, freed my hand, and hurried down the ladder.

It was duak embasan mama back to my home. Emian was excited about the experiences I had enjoyed. I was surprised to learn Emian had also met the Major; she had gone there with her parents before we were married.

Our happy life, working on our kaingin together, was resumed, with the valued help of Emian's parents. Entas and Yawi treated me as affectionately as Agaw and Yonay had, like true parents.

For our first crop we planted corn and some rice. After three months of endless weeding, our field was bursting with tender young corn, an irresistible attraction to the monkeys who visited at night to feast. They can cunningly evade any trap devised. Almost every day I returned to the house furious from discovering a wizened-face monkey squinting down from an unreachable branch, where he sat eating an ear of corn.

Buhid custom obliges the owner of a kaingin to invite others to share in his harvest. To disregard this old custom is considered the basest display of selfishness. After Entas saw the destruction inflicted by the monkeys, he suggested that we harvest what was left of our crop immediately, by ourselves. He assured us everyone would understand the situation.

Despite the meager results, we were proud of our first harvest. It was only a few days afterwards that Emian and I were toiling to expand our kaingin. We had to work fast before the rains became too heavy. While I concentrated on the main crops, Emian labored at planting vegetables and banana plants near our hut. Entas helped me reinforce the roof for the rainy season, only a few months away.

The idleness of the rainy season was almost harder to bear than the heavy tasks on our kaingin. Sporadic visits by Emian's relatives and friends gave us relief from our confinement. I particularly liked the days her girl friends came. Emian and I quickly shrugged off our adult roles and played the frolicsome games of children under fifteen, which was what we were.

Emian's mother, Yawi, came one wet day with her portable weaving loom and a large supply of cotton to teach Emian how to weave. The Buhids raise their own cotton for clothing. It is not known where they obtained their first cotton seed, or who invented their portable loom, or even taught them how to weave. Their clothing material is coarse and very durable.

Emian and her mother were soon engrossed in woman's talk, so I went out to check on our crops. Enjoying the fresh air after the rain, I walked to the far end of the kaingin. I was jolted by the sight of a huge wild pig with two fierce tusks, thrashing about with loud, violent grunts. I finally realized that the beast was caught in one of the traps Entas had helped me set. I slowly recalled what Entas had told me about hunting and trapping baboy talons.

I was reassured by touching my bolo slung from my waist. Entas had insisted I always carry it with me, because wild pigs will attack when cornered and can kill you. However, I could not be too quick with my bolo, for Entas had also told me if I used an iron weapon to kill a trapped baboy talon, the trap would never again catch a pig. Only a wooden weapon would do for killing a snared pig. Fortunately, the wind was blowing away from the trap; if the baboy talon smelled me, in rage and fear he would certainly break the vines that held him.

Killing that baboy talon was too much for me to handle alone. I ran to Entas's house, but he was not there, so I returned to my own hut. When I told Emian and Yawi the news, Yawi urged me to go back and watch the baboy talon, while she ran to get Entas and Paladan to help me.

I took Emian back with me; I knew she would want to be there for the excitement. We kept a safe distance from the baboy talon because he was furiously attempting to break free.

Entas, Paladan, and Yawi were all panting when they arrived. We kept ourselves behind a tree so we could climb fast if the baboy talon escaped. Paladan stood near us with his spear ready, while Entas searched for something to use as weapons. Entas came back with two branches. He trimmed a point on one end of the thinner branch for Paladan to use as a spear. The heavy branch he kept as a club. He moved cautiously until he was within an arm's length of the baboy talon.

With careful steady aim, Entas brought the club down with the full force of his body behind the blow, but he missed. The beast, more terrorized than ever, made a ferocious and desperate attempt to free himself, growling and snorting. The next blow was so hard that when it hit the baboy talon it killed him. That was the biggest baboy talon I ever saw.

With dexterity Entas tied the four legs together and inserted a long pole between the body and the legs so he and Paladan could carry the prize home. His quick, skillful motions showed his long experience in capturing wild animals. A group of friends were waiting at our hut to congratulate us on our successful catch. I was beginning to feel like a grown man. A poncion was planned for the next night, to feast on one of the chief enemies of our kaingin.

While we could set traps against the monkeys with some success, we were defenseless against the greatest single menace to a rice crop, the birds. Here again, Entas had a method for permanent riddance. He was not the least disturbed by the flocks of birds feeding on our rice stalks. Instead of chasing the birds, he asked where our Binhaven was located in the field. I pointed it out to him. Nodding his head, Entas assured me he would be back the next morning to drive the birds away from our rice field forever.

After a field is planted, the bayong that contained the rice seedlings is placed where the planting was started and is enclosed with logs. The meter circling that bayong constitutes the Binhaven, and this site is inviolable to all until after the harvest, except that it may be entered for a purpose specific to the harvest.

True to his promise, Entas came to our hut early the next day. At his instruction I stayed on the edge of the field, while he went directly to the bayong inside the Binhaven. I saw him remove what looked like tree bark and small twigs from the piece of vine tied around his waist. He than sat down, which concealed his actions. A few seconds later I saw smoke rising from the spot where he sat. Rejoining me, he whispered, "Now watch this."

As if responding to Entas's words, the birds shot off in a thick flock. Entas promised me we would never again be pestered by birds in our field, although he would not reveal his secret.

Our next harvest was so fruitful we invited ten others to join us. It lasted for two full days.

I was so happily in love with Emian that I asked her if we might have a baby when we became old enough to produce one. She refused absolutely, saying that if she ever had a baby she would bury it. It is a common, though secret, practice among couples who do not want to be burdened with a baby to bury it when it is born.

When giving birth, a woman does not permit anyone to assist her or even remain near her. She goes into the bushes to labor in solitude. Only after the baby cries will her husband come to wash the baby and its mother. The wife cuts the umbilical cord and returns home with the infant, while the husband remains at the scene of the birth to bury the placenta.

If the couple chooses not to keep the baby, the mother buries it at birth. If only the wife elects not to keep the baby, she suffocates it with the placenta before its first cry and tells her husband the baby was born dead.

---

3 It Takes Seven Days to Bury the Dead

I welcomed Emian's suggestion that we visit her parents; I had real affection for them. I was happy to find Emian's younger sister, Banglad, and her husband, Rausig, also visiting.

Rausig and Entas were discussing their plans for the next planting, the very topic I had come to discuss, too.

This conversation was disrupted by the arrival of two men who remained on the fantao where they unloaded their bolos and bayongs. In a surly voice one of them informed Entas, who met them in the doorway, that they came to find "two female puppies, one of whom was older than the other."

"It all depends what you mean," Entas replied. "I can say yes, or I can say no." Entas asked if the puppies in question belonged to them. The spokesman admitted they did not own the two puppies, but the other man added that the puppies had entered their yard, had been fed, hence, they believed they had a claim on them.

To Entas's question whether the two puppies were leashed, the first speaker without the least trace of reluctance admitted they both knew the "puppies had leashes." With visible irritation, Entas challenged their motives in feeding two puppies they knew belonged to someone else. Their response was so insolent, Entas could no longer conceal his vexation, saying, "Let's stop talking in riddles. Are you referring to animals or persons?"

"We are talking about your daughters," the first speaker replied.

Trembling with rage, Entas summoned all four of us to the fantao. While Entas had been talking to the strangers, Rausig and I sat near each other, and our wives sat across from us. All conversation had ceased as we listened intently. I was seething at the brazen remarks against such innocent girls. Never in our eleven months together had Emian ever deceived me. Rausig was bewildered. The girls remained silent. My heart went out to them in their shock.

To my surprise both men were familiar to me; I had seen them at several poncions I had attended. The older one was Maayhay from Balogbog; the other was Bogtai from Ruspusan Cabog.

When Entas confronted Emian and her sister with the charges made against them, Emian embraced me and Banglad embraced Rausig. Both girls accused the two of lying. Entas angrily unsheathed his bolo and ordered Maayhay and Bogtai to each pay a fine of one depa of panaongens to all four of us to alleviate the disgrace we suffered from their false charges.

That was a severe fine. Mangyan fines usually consist of so many arms' lengths of panaongens. A depa is the measurement from the left shoulder, across to the right shoulder, and down to the tip of the middle finger of the outstretched right hand.

I watched keenly as the two men reached for their bayongs to get the strings of panaongens. My eyes stopped at the inscriptions woven into their bayongs in black vine. One of the bags bore the words "Emian-Maayhay" and the other "Banglad-Bogtai." the bayong with Emian's name was the one I had seen her working on during the rainy season. I tried to conceal my shock. I insisted on giving the panaongens I received from Maayhay and Bogtai to Emian, as a gentle taunt. In the days that followed I tried to evade thoughts of Emian's deception by devoting all my time to our kaingin. Emian would join me, laboring with the same vigor I had so admired. I deliberately established a routine that kept us from having intimate contact. After supper I would fall asleep right away, and would leave the house early every morning. We planted the entire kaingin with corn. In order to complete the planting in a single day I asked Banglad, Rausig, and others to help us.

Rausig came alone. He always worked in the same area where Emian and I were planting. This was the first time I had seen Rausig since the incident. When Emian returned to the house to prepare the noon meal, Rausig told me he had also seen the inscriptions, and that he knew I had seen them. I was silent, hesitating to reveal my own feelings. He went on to tell me about his conversations with Banglad. She had denied any intimacy with Bogtai, but he had insisted that if she was interested in Bogtai, he would grant a separation and set a fine. This threw me into consideration of my own situation. If Emian frankly admitted her interest in Maayhay, Buhid custom dictated that I give her up, but a separation under those circumstances would require Emian and Maayhay each to pay me a fine, I to determine the amount. If, to show my affection for Emian, I imposed such a heavy fine that neither could pay, it would be a means of preventing a separation. Maayhay could not protest the severity of the fine, because Buhid custom stipulates that the fine the husband imposes is final. If

27

neither could meet the fine, Emian would be obliged to stay with me, and Maayhay to seek no further encounters with her. Had the allegations made by Maayhay and Bogtai been proved to be true, Rausig and I could have fined each of our wives heavily. Infidelity is considered a very serious offense by the Buhids.

Rausig jarred me from my reverie, stating that he had a plan. He vetoed, as being childishly stupid, my suggestion that we divorce and then marry two other girls. Rausig was older and more worldly than I. He pointed out that if we separated without any proof of infidelity we would be forced to pay a fine to Entas for leaving his daughters without any real cause. Hence, Maayhay and Bogtai could then marry the girls without any fine whatsoever. Rausig offered the plan that we try to catch our wives in an adulterous act. This would be sufficient reason to demand a separation, and the men would have to pay us a fine. Rausig's argument was persuasive, so I agreed to take part.

A poncion was to be given in a few days to commemorate a friend's death. Rausig's suggestion was to tell our wives we would all attend together. He was sure the girls would use the occasion for a tryst with their lovers. Rausig and Banglad visited us the next day to plan for the trip to Yanao's house for the poncion. The journey would take one-half day of steady walking. Rausig and Banglad agreed to stay overnight with us so we could set out early the next morning.

While the girls got food from the kaingin for our evening meal, Rausig outlined his plan for trapping Emian and Banglad with their lovers. He showed me a torch he had borrowed from Paladan. It made a strange light by merely pushing a button. It needed no fire to make light.

During the meal, Rausig told us of Entas's suggestion that he and Banglad establish a kaingin and build a hut close to ours. Emian and I welcomed the idea. We all agreed they should move in with us until they were settled. It was decided they would move in when we returned from the poncion.

We talked little because we had to walk single file. We trudged up, over, and down so many hills that I lost count. After crossing several creeks, we stopped at one to eat and rest. During the meal Rausig told us the amusing story of

Anagon's adventures in Manila with the Major. This was the first time I had heard about Chief Agaw's son going to the great city.

Anagon had become so unhappy in the city that he came back to Siangi with the Major after only two months. Though Rausig had not seen Anagon since his return, several of Anagon's stories about the strange ways of the Logtanons in their forest of tall, stone buildings had reached his ears. The most popular story was the one about the crisis in the Major's house when Anagon attempted to relieve himself. Shortly after his arrival at the Major's house in Manila, Anagon went behind a shrub in the garden to squat. This promptly caused one of the Major's houseboys to march Anagon into the house, shove him into a small white room, and close the door. Anagon was told that whenever he wished to squat for a bowel movement he was to come into that white room and sit over the open hole of the seat until he was finished, and to keep the door closed. The houseboy's final, emphatic instruction was that Anagon must push down on a shiny, metal handle above the seat when he was through. He preferred to go behind the bush but was afraid to be discovered. Anagon went through the drill just as instructed, but in the process water splashed on his buttocks. Noticing a roll of soft paper hanging on a metal device on the wall, he used most of it to dry himself. He threw the wet wads into the open hole of the seat. Diffidently, he pushed down the shiny handle, only to hear a frightening noise. Very soon, he was almost paralyzed with fright when gushing water overflowed onto the floor. He was convinced that he had broken the thing, so he quietly made his escape. He soon heard loud shouts from the houseboy, who had discovered the devastation in the white room. Under cross-examination he denied any knowledge of the accident, fearing he would be fined a staggering sum for the damage.

From that time on Anagon avoided the white room. He waited to empty his bowels until late at night, when everyone was asleep. He would make his discharge into some layers of paper, wrap it up, stealthily search out a garbage can at a safe distance from the Major's house, and drop it in. His loss of sleep and fear kept him in a constant state of anxiety. It became the main reason why he wanted to go back to Siangi.

After a hearty laugh at Anagon's ordeal, we set off again, reaching Yanao's house at dusk. Yanao's poncion was given as part of the Fafituwan Fag Sirang Kati Kanatoy—Seventh Day Memorial of a Death—in honor of his wife who had died six days before. The crowd around Yanao's house was anxious for the ceremony to begin. Everyone was watching the tiny funeral hut—bahay bahayan—about four-by-five-feet, a meter off the ground, and without walls. It was built near the house where the person had died. All personal possessions were placed in it. Just as soon as Habog and Yanao went to the bahay bahayan the poncion would commence.

The ceremonies for a deceased person actually begin on the day he dies. The moment that death is certain, a relative makes it known by a loud shout. Relatives lay the body in the center of the house in which the person expired, and place on the body layers of tree bark up to one foot high. The clothes worn by the deceased are never removed. The Buhids believe his spirit will roam the earth forever if his clothes are removed. The yard of the house where death occurred is surrounded with stakes of sharpened bamboo to prevent the evil spirits from entering and stealing the body. The burial takes place the next day; the body, having been wrapped in a mat especially woven from buri, is carried to the forest where relatives have dug a grave. Only those who were present at the time of death, or a relative if the person died alone, are allowed to carry the body. It is carried in a large, basketlike container, which will not be placed in the grave. The bottom of the grave is floored with slats of bamboo, so the body will not touch earth; a cover of similar slats is placed about one foot above the body, with wooden reinforcements to prevent the cover from collapsing when dirt is shoveled in on top of it.

Custom permits only members of the family to fill the grave. When finished, all present return to the house where each is given one short string of beads in appreciation. Those who were inside the house at the moment of death are obliged to stay there the seven days. They cannot leave the house or communicate with anyone outside, once they have buried the deceased.

When they find a death is imminent, most Buhids leave quickly to avoid confinement. If, in leaving, any particle of the clothing worn by the departing person touches the house, he is morally bound to stay through the total confinement period. If he violates this tradition he is ostracized by the community, even by his own relatives, for a long, long time.

Relatives bring food and water, leaving it just outside the fence. On the fifth day fanlahiyans go into the yard with a chicken, its feet tied by a piece of vine. The fanlahiyans chant prayers as they drag the chicken in a circle around the house. When the services are finished, the chicken is killed and fed to all who witnessed the ritual. The prayer chanters leave to return the seventh day.

We arrived on the seventh day. I saw Habog and his son, Yanao, come down from the house where they had been confined, and walk over to the bahay bahayan. Two men, presumably relatives, went and stood directly behind Yanao and his father. Neither of them looked behind them because if anyone who has been confined looks directly into the face of another person before the seventh day is officially concluded, it will cause a death soon in the family of the person he faces.

Habog escorted his son past the staked fence to the pigsty. Here Yanao dragged out a large pig on a leash (previously placed there by relatives) and gave the leash to a prayer chanter, who in turn handed it to a relative standing behind him. The relative announced to Habog and Yanao that the pig had been delivered to him, which both men acknowledged by a rigid nod. They then recited an incantation which told Yanao's deceased wife that because of the gift of the pig she was not to annoy the surviving members of her family. The incantation also told her that this pig and the other pigs and chickens to be butchered and served at the poncion that evening, were available to her as well, to take on her journey to the Land of the Rising Sun.

When Habog and Yanao had completed their incantations, the prayer chanters came up from where they had been standing by the bahay bahayan, took the leash and walked away, half dragging the pig behind them. A group of friends, who had to be widows or widowers not yet remarried, walked over to Habog and Yanao, placing before them some especially prepared food, small bits of the meat of wild animals. The servers started serving them this meal, chanting incantations as they did so.

At the conclusion of this ceremony, Habog and Yanao were

escorted back to the house without speaking to anyone. Then a relative announced to all assembled that the ceremony was officially concluded. Habog and Yanao were escorted out of the house, and mingled with and spoke to those present. The poncion started immediately. The food was savory and plentiful.

---

4 Infidelity: Make a Scene or Ignore It?

After we had eaten, Rausig whispered to me that we should now put our scheme into effect by finding a place to lodge for the night. The first house we approached belonged to a woman who had attended the poncion, so she agreed readily. When she suggested that we return to the party but come back later, Emian concurred so quickly as to be revealing. Obviously she was not aware of the trap we were setting.

Pretending a headache, Rausig said he wanted to stay and go to sleep right then. I urged the girls to return to the party, while I stayed with Rausig. The girls quickly agreed. After they left, Rausig and I stealthily departed. We used the marvelous hand-light sparingly to find our way, not wishing to expose our presence. The only other lighting came from tree sap torches strategically placed in the area of the poncion. We could not see the girls anywhere. I was ready to give up the whole idea of entrapping them in anything, but Rausig deduced that because they were not at the poncion, they must be in some secluded spot with their lovers.

We started to check out a cluster of abandoned huts nearby. We sidled up to the nearest and listened for any conversation or movement. All was silent in each hut. But voices in the fourth hut were clear before we even got to it. After listening for only a few minutes, we recognized both Emian's and Banglad's voices. Nor was there any doubt about the male voices. Maayhay and Bogtai. Tears came to my eyes as I suffered the revelation. Rausig flashed his light into the hut. In that brief second I saw a sight I would remember every time Emian came close to me. Lying on mats on the floor were the two girls in the firm embrace of their lovers.

After we left the hut, Rausig and I went directly to the house where we were staying. I selected an isolated corner to lie down. There were many tormenting questions I wished to be alone with. Rausig cautioned me not to let Emian know what we had seen. We tried unsuccessfully to fall asleep. It was much later when the girls returned. Rausig and I pretended to be asleep.

We woke early the next morning and left quietly, so as not to disturb the others. The room was full of sleepers. Outside, fire leaped from Yanao's place, but Rausig assured us it was not an accidental fire. Yanao and his father were burning down the house to prevent the death spirit from lingering behind. Without a house to stay in, it is believed that the death spirit will remain with the dead.

We sought out Habog to say our good-byes. We explained that our wives were daughters of his old friends, Entas and Yawi, who could not come because of the long trip. Habog gave us pork for our trip, as well as a large piece for Entas and Yawi. He was dispensing it to all those who had helped, the largest to the men who had dug the grave.

Except for the delicious meal of cooked pork, our trip was uneventful. We reached Entas's house about mianit kalimbaba. Entas and Yawi received the gift of pork, but were more interested in news we brought about all the people we had seen. Yawi prepared the pork, while the girls were sent to dig some gabi.

I was recounting the amusing story about Anagon's visit in Manila, when Entas's attention was distracted by two men approaching the house: Maayhay and Bogtai. Maayhay addressed me because I was on the fantao near the ladder. He announced they had come to "pick up the two bundles of black vine" they had left behind on their last visit.

All three of us knew what they meant. In answer to Entas's obvious question, Rausig denied having seen Maayhay or Bogtai at the poncion. The girls returned with the gabi before Entas could question me. Emian's explanation to her father was so evasive that Entas realized his daughters had been lying. He then pressed Rausig and me to tell him the truth. We finally told him what we had seen in the abandoned hut during the poncion. Maayhay stated he wished to marry Emian,

33

and Bogtai wanted Banglad. Entas firmly opposed the idea and refused his consent absolutely.

Although a Buhid girl can marry without her parents' consent, she and her new husband must pay a heavy fine, or the parents will never recognize the man as their son-in-law. Emian interceded, saying that since Entas refused his consent, she would pay a retribution of two arms' lengths of panaongens to me, and Maayhay should match the fine. Banglad said she and Bogtai would offer the same to Rausig. After a brief conference Maayhay and Bogtai agreed. The panaongens Emian paid me were the very same beads I had purchased for her from the surplus of our first harvest.

Bogtai then reminded us that he and Maayhay had paid a depa to the four of us during their previous visit. The charges that they had unjustly accused the two girls of infidelity, and for which they had paid, having now been proved erroneous, would dictate the return of the panaongens. Without argument, Rausig and I returned the two depas. They then requested that we not feel animosity toward them. We agreed. The matter was now between Rausig and me and our wives. The amiability with which the matter was resolved did not affect Rausig's or my true feelings. We had both been deeply disillusioned.

We left Entas's house early the next morning for our own hut. Rausig and Banglad were going to be sharing our hut. A cold silence remained between us and our wives.

One day the coldness between Banglad and Rausig vanished. They became a loving couple once again. The enchantment of their love worked as a charm to bring Emian and me together again, also.

---

5 Christianity: True or False?

Sharing our home with Rausig and Banglad became a pleasant arrangement. Rausig, older and more experienced than I, was like a brother, who advised me and shared those tasks that required more strength than I had. Banglad and

Emian were close sisters. I had a deep appreciation for Banglad.

The site Rausig and Banglad selected for their own hut was next to ours, so we could work together on our kaingins. We had not fully recovered from the journey to Yanao's poncion when Boscad arrived with a bitlag informing us that Boscad's Aunt Aymay had died. The message sent by Boscad's grandmother, Yaaynan, asked us to come and, further, told us that our pig, for which she was caring, had been donated to the poncion for Aymay's Fafituwan Fag Sirang Kati Kanatoy. When Rausig and Banglad returned from work, they agreed to join us for the trip.

The next afternoon Rausig saw Entas and learned that he and Yawi had also been notified. Entas asked us to help him carry his two youngest children to the poncion. Exactly at dawn we arrived at Entas's house. Both little girls were awake and excited about the trip. Emian and Banglad helped me bind Ande, two years old, into the broadcloth harness I put across my shoulders and under my armpits. Rausig carried Honay, three years old, in a large vegetable basket. Although we left before Entas and Yawi because of our burdens, I was surprised to learn from Yaaynan that they had not arrived ahead of us. Yaaynan explained that she was not confined because she had not been with her daughter, Aymay, when she died.

Emian and Banglad were happy to see their girl friend, Alot, with whom they had grown up. At Emian's insistence she, Alot, and I made a special greeting ritual called *pasaruk luban gamat*. Emian placed Alot's right hand on top of mine, and placed her own right hand over Alot's; Alot placed her left hand on top of Emian's right, and my left hand went over Alot's; Emian crowned this pile of hands with her left.

It delighted me to find Agaw and Yonay at the poncion, and I introduced Emian to them. Seeing the many people who wanted to pay their respects to Chief Agaw, Rausig and I drifted away. We wandered around glancing flirtatiously at the prettiest girls. I nudged Rausig when I saw a Logtanon boy who seemed very familiar. Casually, Rausig dismissed him as just a Logtanon, there to observe a Buhid affair.

"No, Rausig," I said, "he is not a Logtanon. I'm sure you know him." Before we got close, the Logtanon boy called my name. It was Anagon, back from his famous trip to Manila. We embraced. I was elated to see him despite his ridiculous Logtanon costume. His clothes reminded me of Rausig's hilarious story about Anagon's ordeal with the white room. I did not refer to his stay in Manila to save him embarrassment. I was pleased to hear he and his wife were building a hut near Agaw's. I promised to visit them, and left to search for Emian.

We could hear pigs squealing, which was a sure sign the Fafituwan Fag Sirang Kati Kanatoy had begun. All four of us hurried to the ceremony. Aymay's husband, Ronhay, had been the only one in the house when she died. The ceremony was exactly the same as that at Yanao's house. When we had to butcher our pig our wives asked to watch us. With a piece of rope Rausig lassoed the pig's legs, and once it tumbled over, squealing, I sat on it. Seeing I was not heavy enough to hold it down, Emian leaped up and sat next to me on top of the pig. Banglad stood behind us with a lighted torch, and Rausig tied the animal's stubby, kicking legs. Once it was securely tied, Emian and I got out of the way so Rausig could club it to death.

The two girls started a bonfire with the torch. When the fire became a hot glow, I placed over it two branches, which were wet so they would not burn too rapidly. Rausig and I held the pig over the fire until its body was singed. Next, we placed the pig on a layer of fresh banana leaves that Emian and Banglad had prepared while we were singeing it. Rausig deftly butchered the pig with his bolo, while Emian trimmed off the portions she wanted to use for our supper. The girls had a roast pork supper for us after we delivered the butchered pig to Fodok, who was in charge of the cooking. He told Rausig eleven pigs and twice that number of chickens were being cooked for the poncion.

We retired early so we could leave at daybreak to complete most of our traveling before the sun became too hot. Rausig and I were working in our own kaingin by noon. Later that same day we started gathering materials in the forest to build Rausig and Banglad's home. Before a week passed, we had enough materials to start construction. Rausig went to ask for Entas's help; Entas returned with him. The next morning, at sunrise, all five of us were at the site. By dusk we had the four corner posts upright, and all foliage was cleared. By the fourth day the skeleton of the hut was up, and Entas returned to his family. He was sure we could finish the structure by ourselves. The cogon roof was completed in a single day, and Emian took the surplus cogon home as a hint that our own roof needed repair.

Although the walls were not finished, Banglad was anxious to move into the new hut. I asked them to postpone moving for a few days because I planned to visit Agaw, and I wanted them to stay with Emian while I was gone. Banglad consented resignedly. As soon as I could get Rausig alone I asked why Banglad was so eager to move. Reluctantly, he told me Emian had hinted to Banglad at Yaaynan's poncion that she had designs on a boy named Ehit. Banglad was angry at Emian for the disrespect she was showing me in admitting this. I thanked Rausig for his frankness. Rausig and Banglad left to work on their hut. Emian, alone with me, was dear and flattering. It was an effort to conceal my suspicions, after what I had just learned. However, the lightheartedness of our evening meal was still in evidence that night. I told the others I intended to visit Agaw the next day. Rausig could not resist suggesting that I have Anagon tell me the funny story about his encounter with the white room. We all laughed.

From a distance I could see an unusually large crowd in Agaw's front yard. All that I could think on the way up to the house was that something fatal had happened to the old Chief. I was angry with myself for not seeing Agaw and Yonay more often. I found that I was running. Then I heard a familiar girl's voice calling my name. It was Agaw's youngest daughter, Lohena, and she ran up and embraced me. She started crying. Between sobs she told me that Anagon had hanged himself. They had just returned from his burial. I took her hand and hurried toward Agaw's house in the unconscious hope Agaw might refute her news. Agaw saw me as I entered the room. Before I could speak to him, he came over to me sobbing, embraced me, and said, "Your brother, Anagon, is dead." I cried bitterly. Amit and her mother were sitting forlornly in the corner. It pained me to see Agaw's grief, so I went out on the fantao. He had suffered the murder of Baban, and now Anagon. In my reverie, I did not hear Agaw's oldest son, Rahoyan, speak to me. We embraced, and I shed more tears. Rahoyan and I found a quiet spot and I asked him for the details. I recalled Baban's death, which had been disguised as a suicide. All that Rahoyan could tell me was that Anagon's wife, Ramnay, jokingly threatened to return to Occidental Mindoro. Anagon took it seriously, and hanged himself before sunset of the same day. When we were called to the family meal, I ate merely to be polite; everything tasted like bark. Agaw thought I had known of Anagon's death and had come for the funeral. I said I had come to visit Anagon, believing him alive. Agaw made the disturbing statement that if I had arrived one day sooner Anagon would have been so busy entertaining me he would still be alive. I asked Amit where her husband, Oto, was, as I had not seen him anywhere. Yonay answered instead, telling me Amit and Oto were unofficially separated. Oto had moved in with another girl, but had not settled the separation fines with Amit; therefore, their separation was not official.

An impressive number of people came to Agaw's home as the news of Anagon's death spread. Some came to offer condolences and some were curious. Anagon had many friends in the community. That night I did not sleep; many others also stayed awake, talking until dawn. There was a crowd inside and outside throughout the night.

The next morning, I told Agaw I intended to stay for the Fafituwan Fag Sirang Kati Kanatoy. I was confounded when he told me that they no longer celebrated that ritual. He said that he, his family, and even my father-in-law and his wife, had all been converted to Christianity—Omang Ugali. Agaw explained that the Fafituwan Fag Sirange Kati Kanatoy is performed to drive away the spirit of the dead so it will not threaten the living. Instead, the Omang Ugali teach that if you believe in their leader named Jesus, accepting him as your Saviour, you will live again, because "There is no death in Jesus; the dead shall rise again from their graves."

I asked Agaw if he knew the old man, Pokom. The old chief knew him and was aware that he had once been an Omang Ugali, but had lost interest. Agaw was surprised to learn that Pokom was telling everyone the Omang Ugali teachings were false, so I told him the incident that caused Pokom's disillusionment with the Omang Ugali. When his wife died, Pokom, acting on the Omang Ugali's belief, buried her at the foot of the ladder to their home, with one of her arms above the ground so she could raise herself when she returned to life, as the missionaries had promised. He watched that arm night and day for a sign of movement, so he could help her. Several nights passed without any response, but Pokom maintained his vigil. The odor of his wife's decaying body became so intolerable by the fourth day that he left his house, cursing the white people for the false hopes they had peddled.

The only comment Agaw offered was that Pokom apparently misunderstood the teachings of the missionaries. I was baffled that Pokom, who was a wise man like Agaw, was not able to comprehend the teachings of the Omang Ugalis. What chance did someone as ignorant as I have to understand that strange religion? Agaw said the Omang Ugalis teach that the spirit and not the flesh of man rises from the dead. Agaw told me the American missionary would conduct an Omang Ugali service the next day for Anagon and invited me to join his family there.

The Omang Ugali ceremony was held in a building called a church, which had been built by Agaw and other Buhid converts. After waiting a long time for the missionary, Agaw decided he was not coming, and asked his son Lando to start the service. I learned later that Lando had been trained to substitute for the Logtanon preacher. He started with a prayer to their Lord, thanking Him for my presence at that service, also for Amit's presence, at home after a long absence. He expressed how indebted they felt for the many newcomers, and he begged their Lord to take Anagon into His arms, apologizing for his brother's haste to meet Him. He declared that they received great joy from accepting Jesus as their Saviour, and promised the same delights to the newcomers. Lando related a story about Jesus and Lazarus, and told us also how Jesus was nailed to a cross for our sins; and, if we would but repent and accept Jesus as our Saviour, we too would be certain to have life everlasting. I was overpowered by a deep desire to join their religion. Happiness was manifest in everything they said and did, which I could only attribute to their being Omang Ugalis.

During the noon meal, Agaw told Lando and me that the Major had arrived from Manila and he wanted us to visit the Major in the morning, to notify him of Anagon's death and to obtain some supplies. That same afternoon I visited Anagon's grave alone. It was located at the edge of my old kaingin, so made my memories of Anagon all the more painful.

Headed back to Agaw's I met Rahoyan's brother-in-law, Yamo, who was so upset, that I asked him where he was going. He was going to the creek to find Rahoyan's wife, Bonay. She had gone for water and was away longer than she should have been. I joined Yamo in his search. About twenty arms' lengths from the creek, we noticed excited monkeys chattering directly above us. Looking up, we both saw a woman hanging from a lower branch. It was Bonay. I went up the tree and with my bolo cut the G-string holding her. She crumbled to the ground before Yamo could catch her. Jumping down, I placed my ear to her chest to check for any possible heartbeat. Faintly, Bonay's heart was still working, so Yamo and I carried her to the creek. We poured much water over her face, but she was still lifeless. Yamo suggested we take hair from her private parts, burn it with the G-string with which she had attempted suicide, and make her smell these as they burned. Yamo fanned the smoke toward Bonay's face, and I vigorously massaged her feet, hands, and chest. We then poured more water over her entire body and massaged her.

Finally, Bonay began to breathe heavily. I slapped her face several times. She opened her eyes, looked about her, and sat up. Lamenting that her life had been saved, she got up and headed toward home. I told Yamo to follow her at a discreet distance, in case she might try to kill herself again. I returned her bamboo water container to her house.

It was dusk when I returned to Agaw's. I decided not to tell the Chief about Bonay. He was already overburdened. On my second visit to the Major I felt more at ease with him. To our surprise, he had already heard about Anagon's suicide, and was deeply saddened. He asked Rahoyan for all the details of Anagon's death. He gave me a polo shirt, which was too large, but I gratefully accepted it, planning to give it to Rausig. After a delicious meal with the Major, we started our return trip, loaded with the many things the Major had given us for

Agaw. I left Agaw early the following morning for my home. Emian's reception warmed my heart. After I told her of Anagon's tragedy and of my trip to the Major's farm, she informed me Rausig and Banglad had left that morning for Paladan's house to see Rausig's brother.

We visited Emian's parents the next day. Entas already knew of Anagon's death and wanted to learn all the details. That led to a discussion about their becoming Omang Ugalis like Agaw's family. Entas and Yawi were very pleased to learn of Agaw's request that I attend their church services. In response to our invitation to them to join us in our next harvest, they said it was a distinct honor. Entas gave me very valuable advice on how to build a granary hut. They mentioned that Rausig and Banglad had visited them on their way to Paladan's. From a chance remark by Entas, I learned that Rausig's brother was named Eg-hay. The name aroused an unpleasant association, and while I was pondering this Entas stated that he knew what I was thinking. Then it hit me. The principal suspect in Baban's murder was named Eg-hay. Entas warned me to be most watchful of Eg-hay. Yawi said the same thing.

6 Typhoons: Within and Without

I could not sleep that night; all I could think about was Eg-hay. I was sure Eg-hay would be involved in our lives because Rausig was his brother. I had a foreboding Emian would become entangled with him. I never told Emian of my suspicions. Should Emian become involved with Eg-hay, would he dispose of me as brutally as he had Baban? As we went home, I told Emian I would find out what progress Rausig was making on their hut. My true motive for speeding their move from our hut was the fear of Eg-hay's possible presence, but I told Emian we needed the space to store our bountiful harvest.

I spent that afternoon gathering materials for the granary hut. I was relieved to see Rausig and Banglad when I returned. I told Rausig I needed his assistance in the forest. When we were away from the house I told him my true reason for having him come with me. I asked him if he knew of Agaw's accusation of Eg-hay in Baban's murder. Rausig confided he was relieved that I had brought up the subject, but he was not sure Eg-hay was guilty. Rausig further confided that he had another worry. Unbeknownst to me, Eg-hay had met Emian once at Paladan's, and obviously was attracted to her. Because of our friendship, Rausig had warned Eg-hay not to become involved with her.

The next week Rausig and I were kept busy completing his new home, building my granary hut, and working on our kaingins.

On our harvest day, Entas and Yawi arrived first, followed closely by Paladan and his wife, Enom. Paladan complimented us by delaying his own harvest two days to be present at ours. Among those who attended were Habog, Hodiawan, Agromian, and Liknaw, who harvested others' kaingins because they had none of their own. Eg-hay had stayed home to care for Paladan's children.

Our harvest was complete the second day. Entas and Yawi supervised transferring the corn to the storage places we had arranged, and made sure everyone received his share. Paladan and his wife refused to claim their share, saying they had come because they considered Emian and me part of the family. Rausig and Banglad would not accept their share either, because they wanted to repay us for feeding them while they lived with us.

The next day Emian picked the cornstalks that were considered too small to harvest, and I visited Rausig and Banglad who were finishing the walls of their hut. While I was talking to them, the wind blew harder and harder. The clouds darkened unusually fast. I shouted to Rausig, who motioned his alarm.

The wind's direction made me decide to have all of us take shelter in the small hut at our kaingin. I told Rausig and raced back to find Emian returning from the kaingin because of the ominous sky. All of us recognized signs of an oncoming typhoon. In the hut on our kaingin we would have the protection of the hill as well as the forest. I had to shout over the roar of the winds to tell Emian to get blankets and mats while I ran back for Rausig and Banglad. Before I could get ten steps away

Amit, daughter of Agaw and wife of Bag-etan, weaving a buri bag.

I noticed them running toward me. They were not carrying blankets and mats, so I yelled to Rausig to get them, while I ran with Banglad to our hut.

The winds became more furious; we were fortunate that the rain had not started. Rausig returned. Banglad and I scampered down the ladder to him, and we all raced for the small hut where Emian waited for us. It was so dark we found the hut more by instinct than by sight. The downpour started just after we reached shelter; fierce thunder and lightning followed. The rains were so violent they tore through the hut as if it were made of ferns. Emian and I wrapped ourselves in our blanket, as did Rausig and Bangland in theirs. We doubled the

Bag-etan and Emian, second child-wife.

buri mats over our heads. The winds sounded like a million dogs howling at the same time. There was the constant noise of trees crashing and splashing as they hit the ground. More frightening were the savage sounds directly overhead which told us the rivers were flooding. We felt the rain pour down as if we were under a waterfall. Emian and I groped for some shelter from the downpour, and could hear Rausig and Bang-lad doing the same. The four of us squatted together for body warmth. We were still in this position when I awoke; the others still slept. I was glad to see bright light through the wall. Our mats were drenched, but the rains and winds had stopped. It was a brilliant dawn.

When the others awoke, we surveyed the damage. A huge

Banglad, Emian's sister, and husband Rausig.

branch had fallen on the roof, while a smaller one had gone through and just missed Emian. All the treetops looked broken, and many trees were lying on the ground. We were delighted to find that our house, except for a list to one side, would need only minor repairs. Our corn was soaked, which meant we would have to sun it to prevent it from sprouting. Rausig and Banglad went to their hut to estimate the damages. I assured them that I would help them after I got our hut repaired. Emian efficiently prepared breakfast for all of us.

In only a few days we had everything in order and the four of us went to Entas's kaingin for his harvest. We worked only the last day of that harvest, then went to Paladan's for his. The unavoidable meeting with Eg-hay was my foremost concern as

45

Lohena, daughter of Agaw.

we traveled to Paladan's. Everyone there was at work on the harvest, so we joined in. From a distant corner a man waved, and Rausig said that was Eg-hay. We worked ourselves closer to Eg-hay and I studied him before we would meet. He was much taller and older than I, and his left eye was partially closed. In those brief seconds I hated him.

Yawi had thoughtfully provided the noon meal for us. We found a shady spot to enjoy our boiled bananas and gabi. When we finished, Paladan, his wife, Enom, and Eg-hay approached. Closer inspection revealed Eg-hay's half-closed left eye was very bloodshot. Paladan introduced me to Eg-hay. I nodded my head. He saluted with his right hand. We talked about the typhoon. Paladan congratulated me on my success-

46

Lando, son of Agaw, spearing a fish. Lukmay is watching.

ful harvest. Comparing the size of ours to his, I could offer
Paladan a genuine compliment. Our kaingin would fit into one
corner of his. The secret of a large kaingin, Paladan explained,
was to persuade several families to work it together, instead of
having many smaller kaingins. He suggested that Rausig and I
combine our efforts on a single large kaingin. Eg-hay offered
to join us in this bodbodan.

Normally, Eg-hay's offer would have been welcome, but I
could not ignore its implications. My apprehension deepened
when Emian approved with enthusiasm. Paladan and Enom
excused themselves to return to the field. Eg-hay and Rausig
walked back together; Banglad walked beside me, and Emian
followed. We all worked without conversation the whole afternoon. I was so engrossed I did not notice that Rausig and Eg-
hay had moved up to me. I did, however, notice Emian glancing at Eg-hay. As we collected our harvest, ready to haul to
Paladan's house, Eg-hay was especially helpful to Emian.
Banglad scowled. I pretended I noticed nothing.

As we said our farewells, I learned Eg-hay had decided to

visit his brother and would return with us. A glance at Rausig revealed he had not known of Eg-hay's plan.

Enom suddenly embraced me tightly and said loudly, "Paladan and I are very proud of you. We hope you and Emian will never separate." She was obviously telegraphing a message to someone else.

7 Too Many Husbands—I Leave

Our journey home was quiet. It was long past sunset when we reached familiar landmarks, but the bright moonlight helped us find our way easily.

The next morning Emian and I went to our kaingin to clear up the debris from the typhoon and to decide if we could enlarge it. That afternoon Emian took the heling for water. To my dismay Eg-hay carried the filled heling back. When Eg-hay left I expressed my disapproval of another man helping her with housework. Emian tried to justify it. Eg-hay's presence became more and more irritating to me. About a week after he helped Emian with the heling, Eg-hay told me he was starting a kaingin near mine, and asked if he could live with us, so he could be close to his kaingin. I was overwhelmed by his impertinence. I tried to appear calm, and I told him I would have to discuss his request with Emian.

I was unprepared for Emian's consent to Eg-hay's request. Shortly, I knew I had been outwitted. Returning from my kaingin, I saw Eg-hay unloading firewood onto my fantao. My chagrin grew when Emian took some to start the fire for supper. According to the customs of the Buhids of Siangi, whenever a man brings firewood to any woman's home and she accepts that wood, she accepts the man's society. If the woman splits the wood into small pieces, the wood bearer can stay only a short time. If she uses the wood without splitting it, the wood bearer is encouraged to stay longer. If the woman uses all the wood, the wood bearer is welcome to sleep with her, her husband's objections notwithstanding. The husband has two alternatives: he can either share the role of husband with

48

the other man, or he can demand a separation from his wife, and receive a fine from both his wife and the wood bearer. The latter is the more common practice.

Eg-hay ate with us that evening. He slept at Rausig's. I confronted Emian in the morning. The quarrel we had made me so angry I stormed out of the house to work on my ka-ingin.

When I entered the hut for the noon meal, Eg-hay's personal belongings were there. I was appalled when he joined me for the meal. We ate in silence. I went directly back to my ka-ingin. I was in a quandry, and made feeble attempts to work, but I found myself in the small hut, where I sat all day listening to the chirping birds and the chattering monkeys. I ate my meals mechanically, and went to bed and arose early, because I was in a trance.

I went fishing in the creek, where I met Rausig, also fishing, and Banglad washing clothes. They were aware of what was going on and they commiserated with me. That evening when I went home with some fish I found that Eg-hay's firewood had been used up. Eg-hay wasted no time telling me about the firewood. He and Emian would pay any fine I might ask, but if I chose to stay they would have no objections. I remained silent, and Emian called us to supper. I told Eg-hay to eat and to tell Emian I was not hungry. I finally confronted Emian while she and Eg-hay were eating.

Emain explained she had accepted Eg-hay so I would have help on my kaingin. I revealed my suspicions of Eg-hay's role in Baban's murder, hoping to enrage Eg-hay, but I was the one who became enraged by his composed explanation of his innocence. I had hoped my accusation would anger him; instead he offered me his friendship. Emian proposed that we keep our arrangement a secret. I agreed to their terms, but hoped that in time I would be able to cope with this situation.

In the days that followed Eg-hay was ingratiating to me. He was a hard worker; he never complained and was always considerate. He taught me many techniques for trapping wild pigs and wild chickens, and the different methods for catching young monkeys and training them for pets. On our trips home from the kaingin, Eg-hay always carried the firewood to the house. He was so deft at catching fish that we rarely were without some to eat. We became close friends; Eg-hay was so considerate of my lovemaking with Emian that he inspired me to reciprocate; I respected his intimate moments with her. Eg-hay frequently slept at Rausig's house, which preserved our secret. Eg-hay became my confidant, and played such an important part in both our lives that we would have felt a great loss if he had left us. Eg-hay and I agreed that should Emian have a child each of us would recognize it as his own. (It is the Buhid custom that any woman who sleeps with more than one man can demand that each man acknowledge the child as his. We believe several men can cause one woman's pregnancy.)

One day Emian informed us of a harvest in Afnagan that promised to be so abundant that the share the three of us would earn would far exceed any harvest from our own kaingin. We decided to attend, and started out the following dawn to make the long trip to Afnagan.

Our trip to Afnagan was a happy one; we met various friends and relatives as we traveled. These coincidental meetings on the way to a harvest that promised great toil, excited great laughter and loud gaiety. Our lunch-break was a mirthful celebration. We arrived at dusk. More than a hundred people came, an extraordinary number, since it takes only six people to harvest an average kaingin. It is considered a large harvest if more than ten people attend.

Our host for this harvest, Malay-ay, and his two sons, Agnipan and Ehit, are not Siangi Buhids; they are Lia-bles, who have made great advances in their agriculture. They use carabao and plows, which is revolutionary compared to the Siangi Buhid methods. The Lia-bles settle permanently in the areas they cultivate. The Buhids are nomadic, and to the annoyance of the forest rangers—monteros—they destroy trees and other foliage in making new kaingins.

We presented ourselves to Malay-ay, who knew Emian's parents. Emian introduced me as her husband and Eg-hay as the brother of her brother-in-law, Rausig. Whilte conversing, Emian's eyes focused on Malay-ay's son, Ehit. Malay-ay made arrangements for all three of us to stay with his son-in-law, Wy-dinan. I was abashed by the coquettish behavior of Emian and Ehit. Malay-ay took me aside on his fantao to say that he had assigned us to the house furthest from his because he had observed the flirtatious exchanges. Climbing down the ladder from Malay-ay's house, I reflected that whatever corn I gained from these distant harvests was a poor exchange for the loss of my peace of mind.

Fortunately the family we were to stay with proved most hospitable. Malay-ay's daughter, Heg-nay and her husband, Wy-dinan, were pleased that Malay-ay's harvest was so famous it attracted people from as far away as Siangi.

We had a few days to wait before the big harvest. Our pleasant stay with Wy-dinan and Heg-nay was disturbed by visits from Ehit. His intentions were so obvious that Wy-dinan alerted me. At the first chance to speak privately, Eg-hay told me he planned to spy on Emian and Ehit. Wy-dinan observed that Eg-hay was absent at the same times that Emian was. If Emian went after water, Eg-hay would volunteer to fetch firewood, and they would both be away for long periods. They returned within a few minutes of each other. Eg-hay's spying bore fruit. He confirmed what was obvious to all. Emian and Ehit were secretly having a love affair. Eg-hay wanted to punish Ehit. I urged him not to tell anyone we knew what was going on, because I planned to resolve the matter with Emian when we got back to Siangi.

The first day of the harvest was sunny, with a fresh wind blowing. All the workers were pleasant and cheerful in spite of the backbreaking work of bending over to cut the rice stalks. We were so absorbed that Heg-nay had to remind us that the lunch hour had passed.

On the second day everyone was just as enthusiastic, but Eg-hay and I noted that Emian left the field early that afternoon. Eg-hay and I helped Wy-dinan and Heg-nay with the family chores. We realized our presence increased the burden of their housework. Eg-hay always brought firewood into the house on his way back from the kaingin. We helped Wy-dinan cut down a large bunch of bananas. He said he would have had to make many trips to get all of them home by himself. Wy-dinan and Heg-nay were a truly happy couple. Watching them together, I was reminded of my happiest days with Emian.

We moved into the plowed area on the third day of the harvesting. I noticed that there were many more people that day.

Emian again excused herself early, claiming a headache. Eg-hay reported to me later that Emian was with Ehit. My distress was obvious. I had decided to leave Emian when we returned to Siangi, and Eg-hay knew it. He argued against it, pointing out Emian's good points, and said he and I could work for a happier life together. I promised to make no decision until I had talked with Emian.

There was only one more day of harvesting and two days of winnowing. The three of us had harvested fifteen bayongs of rice; that left us with five bayongs as our share. During the two days we winnowed, Ehit paid us brief but frequent visits despite his job of measuring and recording the large harvest. His conversations with Emian were brief. Eg-hay and I hoped that this was a sign that the crisis had passed. Emian became her old considerate self.

When Ehit took us to his father for the final tabulations on our share, Malay-ay insisted we have ten bayongs instead of five, so we "would have something to remember them by."

The night before our departure the three of us visited Malay-ay to thank him and say good-bye. Ehit informed his father he was going to Siangi to "catch a dog." Malay-ay asked Ehit to stay because he was needed to work on the harvest, but Ehit argued he would complete his mission in Siangi in one week, and return. Malay-ay pointed out that it would be impossible to "catch a dog" owned by another. Malay-ay told Ehit in our presence that he knew Ehit had designs on Emian. He added that he had a warm regard for me and did not want to see one of his own sons make me unhappy. To spare Malay-ay and his wife any further embarrassment I assured them we would be happy to have Ehit return with us, to repay their kindness. Malay-ay granted Ehit's request. We said our farewells, Malay-ay and his wife invited me to come again, and I promised them I would. I felt as though I were leaving home.

---

8 The Major and His Funny American Friends

I headed back to Chief Agaw in a muddle. The heavy downpour in which I trudged fitted my state of mind. The sun had set when I neared Agaw's house. I debated whether I should tell Agaw about my separation from Emian.

If Amit was still living there, she would expect me to remarry her, as she had proposed during Anagon's funeral. Agaw and Yonay would want this, How could I live with them and ignore their desire, although I no longer felt affection for Amit?

Lohena, seeing me, dropped the firewood she carried, embraced me, and rubbed my nose hard. Yonay came out onto the fantao to greet me. Agaw was away checking his pangati. In the house Yonay introduced me to her niece, Alot, and her girl friend, Laga-an. Both girls were friends of Amit's, and although she was in Tauga, they were staying with Amit's family. I learned that Amit's husband, from whom she was separated, had died.

I heard Agaw speaking loudly to Lando, his deaf son. Both were in the small yard. I waited until Lando finished driving a stake before I greeted them. He was carrying a wild rooster which he tied by one leg to the stake with a thin vine. This was a desirable catch because it could be used to lure other wild fowl. Once tamed, it is staked where wild birds are. A net is put around it. The wild roosters attack it and get trapped in the net. The Mangyans sell these birds to Logtanons, who pay high prices.

Agaw and Lando each greeted me affectionately. That night I said nothing about my separation from Emian. The next morning when Agaw mentioned the Major, I blurted out that I would like to go to Manila with him. Agaw immediately surmised Emian and I were separated. He was astonished at Emian's having three husbands. He was shocked that I had shared Emian with the very man he believed had killed his son Baban. After lamenting the attitudes of modern girls, Agaw condoned my separation. He urged me to tell Emian's parents.

At supper we heard two distant explosions. We hurried out to watch for the brilliantly colored flares that signaled the Major's arrival. The old Chief declared we would all visit his Sindogo, the Major, in the morning.

Agaw's attendance made that visit more eventful than any of my previous ones. An impressive number of his relatives turned out to make the visit with him. Chief Agaw solemnly saluted the Major. The Major embraced Agaw as a blood brother, and invited everyone present to eat with him. He introduced Agaw to several people visiting him, who came from the United States. One of the white men took several pictures, and was able to show us the pictures almost as soon as he touched the side of his camera.

Agaw's gift of the wild rooster pleased the Major. When he was away from his many guests I approached the Major and asked if he would take me to Manila with him. The Major seemed pleased, but explained that he would give the matter careful consideration the next time he returned. I was elated.

On the trip back home, Agaw kept the rest of us trotting. I had never seen him so exuberant. Seeing his Sindogo invigorated the old Chief.

Lando told an amusing story about seeing the American women swimming in the creek in short pants. One of the women was lying naked on the stones, face down. She was whiter than the whitest stone and shone like glass. Lando was mystified because she dried herself by the sun, when she had a large white cloth to use. Those strange people with their camera and their funny customs fascinated us.

Lando went with me the next day to help clear my kaingin, so that I had the essential work done before visiting Entas and Yawi to inform them of my separation from their daughter. Entas admonished me for not telling them before that the marriage had become hopeless. I could not accept his offer to speak to Emian about a reconciliation.

Next morning I left early to divide our property with Emian. Buhid custom governing the disposition of conjugal property provides that the kaingin and its crop be equally divided. The house is given to the woman.

Emian was feeding the chickens and did not notice me at first. Turning around she saw me, and ran to embrace and kiss me warmly. There was no trace of Eg-hay's or Ehit's belongings. Emian told me she had sent both of them away the day I left her. She thought I had returned to her. It may have been cruel, but I blurted out that I had come only to make a property settlement. Tearfully rejecting my plan, she accused me of making such a suggestion so that I could continue to torment her with my presence. She angrily said she wanted no part of the kaingin, the house, or anything else that might remind her of me. She was determined to move back with her parents. While I was going down the ladder, I could hear Emian sobbing. I vowed I would never again return. I was ready to forget the whole unhappy union.

Awad and her friend Ehay, were waiting for me at Agaw's with a message from Guihit, who had heard about my skill in healing the sick with medicines. When I had first come to Siangi, I met a renowned medicine man—fangamlang—named Balud. I was so impressed by his skill that I asked him to teach me his techniques. He finally let me accompany him on his sick calls. Balud taught me many of the exorcisms—daniws— for ridding the human body of the evil spirit—fagablang—that causes most ailments. He taught me how to diagnose an ailment so as to choose the right daniw, as well as which spots on the body to massage while reciting the daniw. He also gave me many formulas for making medicines.

Lando went with me to Laksi where Guihit lived. We had to push through the crowd inside Guihit's house to get to the patient. Although Guihit's foot was severely swollen, I could find no wound. Ignoring the pain it caused Guihit, I checked the entire swollen area to find the exact spot of pain. I asked one of the men to dig up the root of a particular bush, while Lando got bark from a certain type of tree. One of the women present boiled them, and then pounded them into a mixture with an oil I had brought with me. After washing Guihit's foot I applied the compound and wrapped the foot with a clean G-string, concluding the treatment with a daniw.

A short time later Guihit said he was feeling relief from the pain. Further treatment would be required, but it was so crowded in his house I could not stay the night. Ehay invited me to her house, where Awad was also staying. We had so much in common; Ehay was separated from Lando and Awad was separated from Dagon. Midway through supper came a message that Guihit was suffering a recurrence of severe pain.

A quick examination of Guihit's foot showed a great swelling, with a small circle of white in the center. With a sharp red-hot knife I punctured the center. Several small splinters of bamboo were discharged. It was clear to all those present what had happened to Guihit. He had built a trap for wild pigs by digging a hole and putting pointed bamboo stakes at the bottom of it. Apparently, a fagablang was injured by the stakes; hence, the fagablang wounded Guihit in retaliation. Wounds inflicted by the fagablang are difficult to heal, because there is never any mark on the body. The fangamlang has to feel for the suspected penetration, which is usually revealed to him through a certain daniw.

I washed the opening in Guihit's foot with the water in which the roots and bark had been boiled. Free of pain he was soon asleep. I returned to Ehay's hut and lay down beside Awad. We were soon making love. Awad was just fourteen and was now my third wife. In the morning when Lando, Guihit, and others discovered I had spent the night with Awad, they correctly surmised we were married. Guihit announced he would give me a gift, a G-string; I accepted it as a wedding present, because fangamlangs cannot accept any form of payment for their services.

The next morning, Awad and I left for a journey of one and a half days to Fontan, to tell her parents about our marriage. Neither of her parents had known she had separated from Dagon. In response to her mother's questions about who I was, she quickly stated that she had separated from Dagon and I was her new husband. Without acknowledging my presence, her mother, Yanomay, plied her with many more questions. At the conclusion of Awad's answers, Yanomay asked me if I was from Siangi. I told her the names of my parents; they sounded familiar to her. Yanomay then asked me the amount of hinoyo I had brought. Awad interposed that she had not requested hinoyo because I had nothing to give. At this point her father returned. His name is Dignay. He was more inquisitorial than even her mother. When he was finally convinced I was Awad's husband, he would only say, "Well, if you are really Awad's husband, make yourself useful. Go get some firewood."

The next morning Awad told me that her parents had left the house early, to go see a man named Tipay to ask about my background. Her parents objected to me because I was small, dark-skinned, and ugly, and too young to support her. At that point Dignay stormed into the house. He and Yanomay had learned I was the son of Tipig of Mayoma, thus I was the grandson of Homnan. My grandfather had allegedly betrayed their chief, Malaynan, to the Japanese during the war. Their custom entitled Dignay to seek revenge from any living descendant of Homnan's for the wrong he had done. In fact, he had a legitimate right to kill me. Further, Dignay informed me that Malaynan's family were demanding my life. Instead, he had somehow persuaded them to allow me to pay a fine of fifteen hundred pesos. Dignay's suggestion that I earn the "fine money" by working on his kaingin was as unreal as the fine's amount, a staggering sum.

At first Awad volunteered to assist me, but gradually she estranged herself. In a short time she informed me she was separating from me, to marry a man named Bitang. Her parents welcomed her decision, and it gave me an escape from my bondage. I reminded Dignay and Yanomay that under our tribal law they were equally as guilty as Awad in bringing about our separation. Therefore, I had the right to impose a severe fine on each of them, but rather than accept such compensation now, I decided to leave. I told them I would inform my foster-father, Chief Agaw, of their slander against the memory of my grandfather. Once he exposed their falsehood, I intended to impose a fine against each of them. I stalked out of their house, never to return.

---

9 Flight from Fontan

Leaving Fontan, I walked back toward Siangi that night through the silent forest. The moonlight was so bright I felt safe among the sharp deep shadows behind jutting rocks and towering trees. Roosters were announcing dawn when I neared Bognay's house. I lay down under a bush, so as not to disturb his family before daybreak. The soft cool earth was a welcome bed and I was soon asleep.

It was well after sunrise when Bognay awakened me, urging me to come into the house. He was concerned that Awad was not with me. I told him I would explain everything later.

Inside the house I saw his wife, Wingay, lying on the floor

awake, but looking pale and weak. She had been ill for three days, I was told, with symptoms I decided were severe diarrhea.

Bognay was on his way to fetch a fangamlang when he happened upon me under a bush. Recalling my reputation as a fangamlang, he appealed to me for help. At my request, Bognay went to the nearby woods and got leaves and root tips from a duhat tree. I washed these ingredients and boiled them, giving Wingay a cup of the broth to drink. I told Bognay to repeat this medicine every few hours, while I took my famahowayon. I wanted to rest first so I would be fresh to observe her symptoms later.

When I awoke, Wingay had recovered enough to sit up and complain of hunger, which is the most reliable sign of recovery. I let her eat a little cooked camote, along with a good swallow of the broth.

I related my ordeal of the past two weeks in Fontan. Both Wingay and Bognay were very sympathetic. I was barely finished when two men who knew Bognay entered the house. They were messengers from Fontan on their way to Siangi, to deliver a message from a sick man in Fontan to his relatives. They invited me to go with them, knowing I too came from Siangi. I did not reply to their invitation to join them in the morning for the long journey. I could not trust anyone from Fontan. The next morning I was away before dawn, while they still slept.

Agaw and his family were finishing their noon meal when I finally arrived at their house. Their surprise at not seeing Awad with me became amazement when I told them we were separated. As I ate boiled bananas I told them about my brief stay in Fontan, and the accusations against my grandfather.

About my grandfather, Agaw could only say that he had not heard that any of our people collaborated with the Japanese during the Great War, although they were tortured and threatened with death if they did not agree to help the Japanese. Agaw promised to look into it, to see if my grandfather was innocent of the charges. He began telling us about his own experiences as a guerrilla during the Japanese occupation of our mountain lands. He had joined the Logtanons although he could not even fire a rifle. But he was able to watch all the movements of the Japanese, who were cutting and hauling away trees in their army trucks. The Japanese had been friendly at first, but they became so enraged because the Buhids were spying on them, that they notified Chief Agaw that any Buhid caught near their camp would be shot; so Agaw stopped the spying activities. Reports reached Agaw of huge iron "birds" filled with men from a very distant land. The guerrilla told him these were American airplanes coming to aid the guerrillas and us. There were rumors that American soldiers had landed on the western side of our island, and these were believed when many Japanese soldiers passed Siangi going South. A guerrilla leader came to see Chief Agaw to thank him for many past services. He explained that their mission was to stop the Japanese from reaching the western section. He asked Agaw for his help. He added that the Japanese were strangers to the area and would not be suspicious of the unarmed, friendly Buhids.

Some time later, under coaching of the guerrilla leader, Agaw approached a group of five Japanese and offered his services as a guide through the mountain footpaths. Agaw concealed a grenade in his right hand, behind his back. When he got near enough he pulled the pin, and threw the grenade at them. He crept up close to four dead bodies. He assumed that the fifth one, a short distance away, was so badly wounded that he would die soon.

The guerrillas congratulated Agaw for his heroism, and said his name would be entered in the records. This was the first time Agaw had ever killed a human being. He was troubled about it, but felt some justification because they had invaded his people's land. Soon after that episode the Great War was ended.

At Agaw's suggestion, I went to work, helping him and Lando in their kaingins. Agaw complimented me on my increased skill in farming. I was pleased to hear his words, which made me feel more manly after my failures in marriage.

One day I was relaxing on the fantao, but I became alert with a shock when I realized the girl I saw coming through the trees was Awad, walking alone. Coming up on the fantao she spoke first, asking to see me alone. Dazed by her sudden presence I invited her into the house, assuring her that Agaw and

Yonay were away, and Lando and Lohena were washing down at the creek. Her first words were, "Bag-etan I come here to return to you." I could not answer. I was prepared to hear any statement from her but that one. Her presence recalled only unpleasant memories.

Buhid custom requires that when either of the separated spouses chooses to return to the other, he or she is morally obliged to take the former partner back, unless such a remarriage would cause trouble for either of them. If so, a refusal is justified. There were many cases in Siangi in which a man had been obliged to separate himself from his more recent wife, even though he had children by her, to comply with the request of a previous wife to be taken back. If the man's current wife consents, the previous wife must accept her as an equal. Two other remedies in this polygamous situation are for the husband to find another man to marry his former wife, or to pay her a heavy fine, such as one pig. For a few moments I debated the vengeful pleasure of rejecting Awad for the wrongs inflicted on me by her parents, but I was impressed that she had undergone a dangerous and humiliating journey from Fontan to Siangi to ask forgiveness and reacceptance.

My denial of her request, while not harsh, was firm. Women seem to believe that since water can reduce stones to sand, their tears can melt any male's firm resolve.

Awad was sobbing when Agaw and Yonay entered the house and saw this strange scene. After Yonay heard Awad's story, she entreated her husband to solve this crisis. Once again Agaw showed his wisdom. He commended Awad for her courage in traveling so far to prove her love for me. This stopped her crying. Agaw then pointed out my justification for denying her request. He appealed to each of us to consider our youth; while our problem might at the moment seem overwhelming, it was an age-old one that had been conquered many, many times. Agaw's wise advice soon had us exchanging understanding smiles.

Coming into the house and seeing Awad dozing in the corner, Lando looked surprised. I signaled him to join me outside. Lando sat beside me on a log near the house, and I explained Awad's presence. It was soon apparent that I did not have his full attention. Following his gaze, I saw two men approaching us, one of whom I recognized as Bitang, Awad's husband.

Lando and I quickly went into the house to alert Awad that her husband was pursuing her. Awad begged that we hide her. The best we could offer was a buri mat to wrap herself in. Hearing the two men on the fantao, I went out to meet them. Bitang looked past me and, in a loud voice, asked if I had seen a "dog from Fontan." I answered that I had seen a "dog from Fontan" pass our house on its way to my cousin's. He asked for directions to that house, which I gladly gave him.

The man who had come with Bitang told me he had a letter for me from Do-ngay, my cousin in Fontan. The message implored me to come back to cure him and his wife, Enes, of a severe illness they both had. It also said he knew of my bad feelings about Fontan, but assured me I had nothing to fear. If I could cure their sickness, they would not tolerate any unkindness to me.

Do-ngay's appeal meant we should leave at once, but Yonay insisted we have a meal before the long journey. Squatting there eating, I was startled when Bitang's voice shouted from the entrance to the house. He demanded to know why the "dog from Fontan" was not at my cousin's house. While talking to me, he was staring at Awad's bare feet projecting from under the mat on the floor. Aroused by his question, Awad came out from under the mat, declaring with anger that she was not his or anyone else's "dog." I informed Bitang I was not in the least interested in Awad. Ignoring me, he demanded that Awad explain her presence in the same house with me. She said she was there to visit Lohena. Bitang left with an ugly look on his face.

---

10 Fontan Revisited: Miracles Performed

The sun was still high when the message-bearer, Anaw, and I bade our farewells before leaving for Fontan. Yonay kissed me, and petitioned her Omang Ugali God to accompany us. Lando asked me in whispers what he should do about Awad. I indicated by signs that I did not care what happened to her. Shaking his head, Lando looked disappointed.

Anaw proved to be a good traveling mate. We soon became friends. As we approached Do-ngay's house I was pleased to see it was outside Fontan. I had no fond association with that village.

Anaw introduced me to Do-ngay and his wife Enes. Joy, mingled with relief, was reflected on Do-ngay's face. Enes, who started to cry when she saw me, told me she had nursed me as an infant. They introduced me to their three daughters, whose ages ranged from seventeen down to ten, and to their only son, Benhi. I tactfully asked if I could examine my two patients at once.

There was a swelling on Do-ngay's back, about the size of two adult hands. He said he had suffered from this condition for eight days, and several times he had had difficulty breathing. Enes said she had been afflicted with a severe pain in her stomach, since the day her husband became ill. Her stomach was so swollen she appeared to be pregnant. I felt it. Her abdomen was as hard as stone. It was obvious that the fagablang had injected a good deal of air into her stomach. I decided to work on Enes first.

The two youngest girls eagerly dug up some ginger. The eldest girl got coconut oil for me. After cooking the oil, I mixed it with the ginger, and applied this salve over Enes's entire abdomen. While very gently massaging her stomach in a circular motion, I recited the same daniw I had used in similar cases. In a few minutes Enes expelled putrid air, and immediately after she had an urge to relieve herself. I continued the massage until her abdomen softened and flattened. Enes soon recovered.

In my reexamination of Do-ngay's back I readily discerned he had been shot with a fagablang's arrow, and that the head was still lodged in him. When I explained what I had found, I asked Do-ngay if he had quarreled recently with anyone, but he could not recall having spoken a hard word to anyone in many years. It was plain that someone who had become angry with him had contacted a magdadaniw to call upon evil spirits to do Do-ngay great harm. I was obliged to appeal to the good spirit—Ilagan—to counteract the injury inflicted by the fagablang.

Several neighbors had gathered to watch me perform my cures. I had to request that everyone, including members of the family, leave the house while I worked on Do-ngay. When alone with Do-ngay I asked him to tell me everything he could about himself, in the hope of discovering why someone would want to harm him. It was my unpleasant duty to inform Do-ngay that if the llagan showed him favor I could cure him; if not, I was powerless to do anything for him. While he was not able to remember any particular argument, Do-ngay did reveal that he held the office of message censor—fanduat surat—for his community. Some people, especially the young men, would occasionally become irritated about his censorship particularly when a message dealt with love affairs. A fanduat surat keeps a box in his home where everyone mails his "messages," to be censored before delivery. The fanduat surat is obliged to read all these messages and eliminate anything that might upset good community relations. The fanduat surat gives them to the local postmaster—famuayong—who assigns each message to a carrier—fandia surat—for delivery. A tamalo writes letters for those who cannot write. All of these offices are performed without compensation. Do-ngay's job as the fanduat surat was the key to his problem. This information armed me to start working on him.

Do-ngay's son was sent to fetch a young rooster and some more coconut oil. My request for a piece of rope, a piece of thin vine, with which to bind the legs and wings of the rooster, and a sharp knife was quickly fulfilled. I tied one end of the rope to the rafter, so the other end was directly over Do-ngay's swollen back. I then tied the bound feet of the rooster to the end of the rope, so its beak pointed to the swollen section, and tied the wings to the rooster's body so it would not flap about. I waited for the moon to set before I started exorcising. When that was completed, I felt the swollen section of Do-ngay's back with my left hand, while holding the knife in my right. Repeatedly I checked the rooster's beak to ascertain that it was pointing toward the swollen section.

While reciting another exorcism, I moved the tip of the knife lightly over the swollen area. Next, I lighted the lamp and found, to my relief, that Do-ngay was asleep. I cut the jugular vein of the rooster, being careful that its blood drained onto the swollen area. Holding the rooster's head with my left hand, I placed my other hand on Do-ngay's swollen back. I blew out the light, and massaged the warm dripping blood from the rooster over the swollen area while I recited the third exorcism. I continued massaging until I located the arrowhead, extracted it, and stuck it into the dying rooster. I massaged the swollen area until the rooster's blood stopped dripping. (An arrowhead in such cases is invisible to all but the fangamlang.)

I heated the coconut oil and massaged it into the swollen spot. After finishing that, I asked one of Do-ngay's daughters to assist me. While the girl was wiping off all the blood and coconut oil from her father's back, I assigned one of the older men to bury the dead rooster. His task was essential because the rooster contained the arrowhead.

I dozed off, to awake to the babble of many voices. I was glad to see that Do-ngay was up and looking much better. By the next morning most of the swelling had gone down, and Do-ngay was able to walk without assistance. From the conversations I had with Do-ngay during his recuperation, I learned the answer to the mystery of my grandfather's conduct during the Great War. My grandfather, whose name was Homnan, was accused of collaborating with the Japanese, but these accusations were never proved. However, he had been tortured by the Japanese to such a degree that he subsequently died. This information more than repaid me for any services to Do-ngay in his illness. At least I was freed from the suspicions about my grandfather.

Do-ngay insisted upon sponsoring a poncion in my honor to celebrate his recovery. He also informed me that he would invite three girls as companions for me. Before the poncion, I received visits from people far and near who suffered from minor injuries and from diseases unknown in all the legends of the fangamlang craft. Some people I was able to cure; others I could only try to console. On a brief walk through the village with Do-ngay's son, I discovered I had become a celebrity. When I later complimented Do-ngay on the number of friends he had, he could not conceal his bitterness toward that person who desired to have him killed by the fagablang, simply because he was performing a civic duty as the town's censor.

Do-ngay was somewhat reassured when I explained he had nothing further to fear from his enemies, and that he had the power to inflict the same injury upon them. On the morning before the poncion an incredible number of people came to Do-ngay's to volunteer their services. Seats were constructed, firewood was piled high, and bolos were sharpened to slaughter the two pigs that would be cooked that night. Some brought gifts of rice, vegetables, bananas, and chickens, to insure the success of Do-ngay's poncion.

By early evening the guests were there, and the village of Fontan was well represented. Do-ngay and Enes circulated among their guests, and their eldest daughter, Solingan, with her sister, Mayang, supervised the kitchen activities.

I was totally absorbed with the mystery of which girls were the three Do-ngay had invited for me to meet. Do-ngay tapped me lightly on the shoulder. Turning around, I saw three of the loveliest girls I had seen that entire evening. After introducing me, Do-ngay vanished. Panay appeared to be about fifteen, Tayuan could not have been more than fourteen, and Homnay was an interesting seventeen. Tayuan and Homnay were from Taguran, a flatteringly long distance for them to travel just to meet the famous fangamlang from Siangi. Except for a few minutes I begrudgingly shared with the adult guests, I was with the three girls the rest of the evening.

Panay invited me to sleep at her house, pointing out that there were so many who would be staying with Do-ngay. Tayuan and Homnay both offered the information that they were staying with Panay.

The flickering sahing inside Panay's house enabled me to discern the figures of people lying all about the floor in deep sleep. With intricate maneuvering, Panay wedged a space for each of us to lie down. Sleep was not my concern. In an intimate conversation with Homnay, I promised to marry her. Tayuan left with Homnay early the following day, and I assured them I would follow shortly.

A few days later, approaching the house I recognized from her description as that of Homnay's parents, I had mixed feelings of curiosity and apprehension at the sight of a large group of people. My first guess was that some sort of meeting was in progress. Seeing Homnay waving down at me, I waved back, only to see all the other people start waving at me.

To my discomfort, I learned that I was the cause of that assembly. The two girls greeted me and escorted me to Homnay's parents to be formally introduced. I was even further embarrased when Homnay's father, Yagay, introduced me to the crowd as "the famous fangamlang" from Siangi, and declared he was going to have a poncion the next day in honor of my visit. Because I had been able to cure a few people of wounds and illnesses through exorcism, people had traveled long distances in the hope and belief I could perform miracles. It was a painful experience for me to tell the parents of one boy, with a horribly withered leg, that I could not possibly help him. I found myself destroying the meager hopes for relief of those suffering from blindness, crippled bodies, and total deafness.

I was moved to tears by the pitiful appeal of a beautiful fifteen-year-old girl, who had been blind since she was twelve. Tears trickled down her cheeks when I explained to her as gently as I could that her affliction was one that was beyond my power to cure.

She begged me to place my hand over her eyes. I did not wish to comply with even this simple, pathetic request; it was too suggestive of deception. She put out her small hands, searching to touch mine. Finding one hand, she clutched it, and before I realized her intent, started rubbing my fingers over her closed eyes. She did this repeatedly, and I could not stop her. Silence fell over the crowd as each watched what the girl was doing. After a few minutes, she let go of my hand and wiped the tears from her face. She closed her eyes for a few moments. Opening them she looked straight at me and then turned her head to look at the others. She cried out, "I can see shadows moving. Bag-etan! You have cured me. You have made me see again!" She ran to me, embracing me and crying with joy.

The girl had regained some portion of her sight, but no one was more astonished than I was. I had done absolutely nothing to cure her blindness. The people were amazed. I could hear them whispering the word "miracle." Realizing the danger of having a false claim to miraculous powers, I told the crowd that if this girl could now see again, I had nothing to do with the cure! It might have been her unshakable faith, or it might have been the God of the Omang Ugalis or the Good

Typical Mangyan youth wearing the long hair that missionaries are trying to discourage.

Spirit, but whatever it was, it did not happen as a result of anything I had said or done. A respectful silence followed my speech, and then someone shouted: "The young fangamlang from Siangi is too modest. Now we know that everything they say about him is true." The people, especially the old women, surged upon me grasping for my hand to kiss it. I learned from Homnay's father that the blind girl had been terrorized by a huge snake that had passed over her feet when she was twelve. She had gone into a state of shock, contracted a fever, and been blind ever since.

I told Yagay I had come there to marry his daughter. He said he would give me his decision after he had discussed it with

67

Mangyan Kiting cooking gabi.

Homnay and his wife, Anaynay. At the evening meal Homnay prepared a sagaba of bananas and gabi, and we both ate out of it. When two lovers eat from the same sagaba in the presence of either set of parents, it is done to declare their love and desire to be allowed to get married. Seeing us eat together, Yagay and Anaynay discussed the possibilities of my marrying their daughter. Yagay told me that I would be Homnay's first husband, although she was seventeen years old, and he did not want her first marriage to be a disappointment. He felt obliged, therefore, to impose two conditions on our marriage: I could not take her away from Taguran; and secondly, we could be married for only a thirty-day trial period. He based his decision on my youth, coupled with the fact that this

68

Design on Mangyan baruka.

would be his daughter's first marriage; hence, if the trial period indicated we could live happily together, then we could be permanently married. Homnay accepted the conditions, so I agreed to them. Buhid parents of an intended bride have the right to impose a time limit on the marriage.

In accordance with Yagay's requirement that I obtain the consent of a blood relative or foster-parent for the marriage, I inscribed a letter to Do-ngay requesting his approval. I explained to Yagay and Anaynay my reason was that Do-ngay lived closer than Chief Agaw. Yagay planned to announce our plans at the poncion.

Yagay showed his acceptance of me as a member of his family by revealing an old family secret. Many years earlier Yagay

Ayaway moving to a new home with all her possessions.

had had a falling out with Chief Agaw over a woman. At that time Agaw was extremely proud that he possessed two wives, and his position in the tribe insured that no one would dare to have designs on either of these women.

A couple of Yagay's friends mischievously goaded Yagay into luring Yonay, Agaw's prettiest wife, away from the Chief, and Yonay had a baby by Yagay, but the child died before it was a year old. The two men became enemies. One day, Yagay suddenly grew up. Realizing that his people needed Agaw's leadership, Yagay persuaded Yonay to return to Agaw. Yonay agreed to go back to Agaw on condition that he detach himself from the other wife. Agaw complied with Yonay's demand,

and was later quoted as saying he was twice as happy with a single wife in Yonay than he had been with two women. Although Agaw and Yagay had never formally reconciled their bad feelings, there was no longer any enmity between them. I was left with the feeing that Yagay's motive in telling me that incident was so I might be instrumental in bringing about a formal reconciliation through a successful marriage to his daughter.

The night of the poncion was perfectly starry, and the fandia surat soon returned with Do-ngay's message consenting to my marriage, in time for Yagay to announce the news as further cause for celebration.

Homnay had her own small hut a little distance from her parents' home, and we moved into it the night of the poncion. We were happy together from the very start. I spent all my spare time repairing the hut. I also helped Yagay in his kaingin, and attended to the medical needs of those who sought help.

Eventually I inscribed a letter to Agaw, telling him of my most recent and happiest marriage. I could picture the sober look on Agaw's face as he read that Homnay was two years my senior and entering her first marriage, while this was my fourth. I touched only lightly on this fact, and stated that what would make this marriage last was my resolution to prove myself a responsible, mature husband, which I knew would make Agaw proud of me. I added that Yagay had informed me of their old quarrel; it was, therefore, my fervent hope my marriage would serve to increase good will between them. I explained that my decision to obtain the required consent for marriage from Do-ngay instead of Agaw, whom I recognized as my foster-father, was because of the quicker reply. I did not tell Agaw of the time limit on our marriage.

Do-ngay's daughter, Solingan, honored us with a surprise visit one day as her father's messenger, to learn how well we were getting along in marriage. She invited us, on behalf of her father, to visit Do-ngay's family. I was happy to learn that Do-ngay was still as healthy as I had left him. However, he continued to be unhappy because someone might use evil spirits against him. Solingan told us her father wanted to resign his position as the message censor because of the ill-treatment he suffered from some vindictive member of his own group, but the older people persuaded him not to.

Each day of our marriage was increasingly blissful. Neither of us found cause to argue. However, our happiness together was threatened during the last week of our trial period. Tension arose because our future happiness hinged on "getting through this single week." It affected our relationship badly. I could not shake the forboding that our wish to continue our lives together would be denied us. I tried to hide my apprehensions from Homnay. The night before the final day of our probationary period Homnay and I discussed what her father's decision might be. I then perceived the first hint of Homnay's uncertainty.

The next morning Yagay stated he had detected aloofness between us during the last week of our probation. It was his decision, therefore, that we should be separated for one month to find out whether our love for each other would outlast such a trial.

When my remonstrances had no effect, I vowed to return to Homnay at the end of the separation. Although Homnay and I parted tearfully, I suspected that she did not desire to continue our marriage and had told this to her father, which was the true reason why he dissolved it.

After my return to Siangi, where I was living with Chief Agaw once again, I received a message from my boyhood friend Hagan, that informed me he was on his way to Siangi and wished to see me.

Hagan arrived one day after his message, and we devoted our first day to reminiscing about our childhood. Despite Agaw's reproachful looks, I eagerly accepted Hagan's invitation to accompany him back to Opay.

---

11 My Lady or My Life

During the two-day trip, we exchanged experiences from the time we had last met. My matrimonial record amazed Hagan, who confided he had trouble keeping his wife in his own bed. His deep attachment to his son, who would go with his mother, prevented separation.

My first morning at Opay, Hagan's wife Maynaynay introduced me to her sister Belen. Belen was living with her Aunt Bonay who, despite the efforts of the local fangamlang, had not recovered from a recent injury by the fagablang. Smitten with Belen's beauty, I offered my medical services, and assured her that I would call upon her aunt that very evening. Anxious to impress her, I explained that a fangamlang worked best at night; otherwise I would have begun the cure immediately.

My examination that night revealed that Bonay still carried two tiny pieces of the evil arrowhead within her. When she and her husband, Talon, had consented, I started reciting a daniw as I tried to remove the pieces. Despite Bonay's writhing, I was successful, and with satisfaction I stuck the pieces in the rafters and left.

Early the next afternoon Belen was at Hagan's with the message that Bonay was up and anxious to see me. Filled with questions, she cornered me. Delighted, I went into a detailed explanation of the fangamlang mystique; that we depend upon the good humor of the llagan for our powers and thus cannot charge for our services. If the llagan feels that a fangamlang is unethical, he can not only take away his power, but may also inflict illness upon him. Belen and Hagan paid rapt attention, and were surprised to hear that a fangamlang cannot cure himself or members of his family. Hagan asked if there were any female fangamlangs; I had heard there were, but had never met one.

Alone for a moment on the fantao, I spotted a necklace in Belen's bayong and took it. According to our belief, if a suitor steals something personal from a girl, it will be much easier to win her, if he knows the proper daniw to recite. Belen fetched her bag for some chewing tobacco and then searched it frantically for the necklace, asking everyone if they had seen it. Of course I denied seeing it, but gallantly offered to search the path. Hagan joined me. I told him what I had done as soon as we were out of sight, and he cooperated. Deliberately, we did not return until it was too late for Belen to leave. As we lingered, Hagan told me Belen had a crowd of young men pay-ing court but she would not make a choice. They would not welcome a newcomer, and Hagan advised me not to add my name to Belen's list of suitors.

At dinner I learned that Belen's uncle had become so fed up with the clutter of young men that he had decreed Belen must make her choice the following night. Belen smiled consent to my request to join the elimination contest.

The next night I arrived promptly. As soon as Bonay had thanked me and praised my medical treatment, I returned Belen's necklace to her. I could sense animosity from the other suitors. Talon ordered us all to sit in a circle, with Bonay standing in the middle. He extracted promises that no grudges would be held against the chosen one, and Belen started cross-examining each suitor. She then announced we would all have to return the next night for her decision. Since several suitors were staying the night at Talon's, Belen returned with us to Hagan's.

When we reached the hut, Maynaynay whispered to me that Belen had made her choice—me. Elated, I accepted the marriage blanket from Hagan, as Belen took the traditional mat from her sister.

Long before the others were awake the next morning, I presented myself to Bonay as she had requested. She wanted me to pick some betel nuts for her. Lot-an, one of the suitors who had stayed the night, offered to show me the nearest betel tree, and explained the local belief that the fangamlang should pick a sufferer's betel nuts or tobacco, so that the ill one would not get stomach cramps.

We came to a river. Just as I was about to cross, Lot-an shoved me hard. He laughed as I climbed out and tried to dry myself. I was angry and suspicious. We found the tree without further mishap. Busily picking up nuts, I felt a sharp pain in my forearm and looked down. Lot-an's spear landed beside me. I grabbed my arm to stop the profuse bleeding, and frantically searched for a cloth to tie around it. I sickened with fear that Lot-an had poisoned the spear, leaving me only minutes to live, and then was overcome with the desire to revenge myself. Leaping up to draw my bolo saved my life. Lot-an just missed crushing my head with a huge branch. As I struck at him, a stranger yanked him out of harm's way, and cuffed his ears hard. Lot-an ran before I could reach him again.

One day as I gathered branches and cogon I heard someone following me. I hid behind the nearest tree and looked around. I saw no one, but hoping that Belen had come after me I called to her. Disturbed when I got no response, I grabbed my bundle of cogon and ran.

Something pierced my bundle. Ducking behind a big tree, I heard a thud as an arrow struck the trunk. Another arrow stuck out of the bundle I carried. Trembling with fear and praying, I listened for footsteps but heard nothing. I threw a small stone away from where I was standing, and pretending that Belen was there, shouted to her not to move. If my archer thought Belen might recognize him, he might panic and leave. It worked. I heard someone running away, and as soon as I was sure of it, I did the same.

Belen, Etang, and I were soon in family council. We agreed that only feuding would result if we brought charges. Etang did, however, take the arrow to see if he could identify the owner. Often it is possible to do so, because materials peculiar to an individual region are used in making arrows.

That evening I relaxed with Belen as we bound the cogon into bundles, as thick as a man's wrist; these would be looped around poles and lashed to the rafters to form the roof. A perfectionist, Belen combed each bundle to remove the dried and broken grass.

The next day we collected cogon until almost dusk. Late as it was, we went to the creek to wash. I was a discreet distance away from Belen, and bathed in a rush, mindful of the late hour. As I hurried back to her, I heard a splash behind me and then a second one. Someone was throwing heavy stones at me. I was relieved to reach Belen and to find her finished bathing. Telling her nothing, I rushed her back to the house.

As I rose the next morning and looked out the door, I found a piece of bamboo stuck under the joists. It read: "You were lucky the first time, but you cannot always be so lucky."

At the noon meal, Etang told us he would return to Opay with us the next morning. I was relieved, since no one would try anything with Etang there. Alone with Belen, I showed her the piece of bamboo. It upset her terribly. Our trip to Opay the next day was uneventful, but at dinner Etang and Belen told Hagan about Lot-an and the bamboo message. Hagan was enraged, but agreed not to press charges.

As soon as Etang left, Hagan and I started working on our hut. With the aid of Talon and Yupak and several others we were finished within a week, except for the roof.

The only uncomfortable moment I had was when someone asked me where I had gotten my skill in building huts. In order to win Belen, whose main objection to most of her suitors was that they had been married before, I had lied and told her I had never been married. Now I had to lie again, and said I had once earned a living building huts.

Belen and I made a short visit to Mianao. This was so peaceful, I began to believe my enemy had decided to leave me alone.

One morning after our return to Opay, Belen and I entered the forest to collect vines for lashing the cogon to the rafters. We were both looking up as we walked, in order to estimate the length of the vines. I happened to look down for a split second, just in time to yank Belen so hard off the path we both fell. Angrily she asked if I had lost my mind. I told her to watch carefully, and threw a branch at the spot where she had been about to step. As the stick hit the ground, a sharply pointed stake shot across the path with such force it embedded itself in a tree. Thinking it a trap I had set, Belen furiously asked why I had not marked it. I explained that I had not set the trap and that obviously it had been left unmarked deliberately. Looking at the trap, we could tell it had not been there more than two days. It was not necessary to tell Belen my enemy was back. She was so angry and fearful that we stopped collecting vines. Without telling her, I looked for a warning sign—a faagap—which alerts people to a nearby animal trap. The way the sign is made indicates the type of trap. There was no faagap, which made it certain the trap had been laid for me.

As we walked home I reviewed everything that had happened, and reluctantly thought of returning to Siangi. My antagonist was going to continue his attacks on me until he succeeded, or killed Belen by mistake. I loved Belen too greatly to risk having her killed.

At the house Belen became hysterical, and I had to tell Hagan and Maynaynay what had happened. Impulsively, I told them I had decided to go to Siangi for a short stay. I pointed out that before it had only been my life that was threatened, but today's incident showed that Belen could be killed accidently. I added that my enemy might come out in the open if I were not around. There was a stunned silence, and Belen drew me close to her. Hagan asked me to show him the trap.

Alone at the trap, Hagan asked me my motives for returning to Siangi. I pointed out what would happen if Belen were killed: Etang would condemn everyone involved with the marriage, and would kill everyone he suspected of having a part in her murder. There was another aspect: should my enemy—who could only be described as a man from Opay—succeed, my friends and relations would seek revenge by striking down anyone from Opay. I asked Hagan if he could imagine trying to explain my death to Chief Agaw.

Hagan agreed it would be safer if Belen and I went to Siangi, but pointed out that Etang would never let her live so far away. Because the problem was so complex, he agreed to help me in any plan I decided on. I told him I would leave for Siangi, ostensibly for a short stay. After I left he could start bracing Belen for the fact that I would not return.

Back at the house, we told the girls I was leaving for a short visit to Siangi. They were skeptical. I urged Belen to return to her father while I was gone, and agreed to meet her soon again in Opay.

---

12 Banished by Agaw

I trudged back to Siangi with a heavy heart. To have to report another broken marriage to Agaw would surely bring his scorn.

Fifty arms' lengths from Agaw's house Lohena rushed up to kiss me. Placing my arm across her shoulder, I walked with her toward the house. Artlessly she asked me where my latest wife was; she had learned from Lando that I had remarried. Before I could finish telling her that we had separated, Lohena accurately predicted that Agaw would be angry. She told me he was away but Yonay was at home. When she met me, Yonay was justifiably reproachful and deeply hurt because I had never shown them respect by introducing any of my wives to them except Emian, at the poncion when Yaaynan's daughter Aymay died. She had decided that I must be ashamed to consider them as parents, or that I lacked sufficient pride in the girls I married. That meeting with Yonay was painful.

I was wandering about looking at the new crops Agaw had planted when I saw Amit approaching with another girl. The other girl's complexion was so fair I first thought it was Awad, until I saw that she was shorter and had a different walk. Amit introduced her as Tinay from Tauga. Blurting out that Tinay had come to Siangi to "tie a chicken," Amit started giggling. Tinay reported that Amit had separated from Yando because he was so overbearingly jealous. She had paid a fine of one depa of panaongens. That was Amit's fourth failure in marriage since she had divorced me. Our mutual failures in marriage gave us something in common.

A slight shadow lay across the room by the time I entered the house to see Tinay alone in one corner weaving a bayong. She told me Amit was asleep in the small room Agaw had constructed for himself when he was so ill. Amit was lying with her back to the door but rolled over and asked me to sit beside her. We were soon caught up in passionate embraces. When we came out a couple of hours later, Tinay gave a convincing performance of being so engrossed in her weaving that she had seen nothing. I excused myself to fetch some firewood for Yonay.

While I was unloading the wood in the kitchen, I could hear Agaw talking with Amit and Tinay. His only response to my salutation was an austere glance. I went outside. I was soon joined by Agaw, who made it clear he wanted a serious talk with me. Without anger, Agaw enumerated my many disgraceful actions, and explained that he and Yonay were kept in a state of anxiety when I was off on one of my crazy adventures. Two weeks earlier he had been obliged to travel to Payagnon to check out a report that I had been found hanging from a tree, only to discover that I had married a girl in that area named Limayan with whom I had quickly established a reputation for attending every poncion given, invited or not. The moral that Agaw was emphasizing was that, since it was known throughout Siangi that I was under his protection, he and his family would suffer intolerable shame if I were killed because of a brainless involvement with some woman. My feeble excuse that I was too young to be as thoughtful as he wished was countered by his statement that whenever he gave me advice, I always claimed to be too young to understand, but I was willing to marry and learn from any woman who wished to teach me.

There was no excuse or answer I could offer. After a long silence, Agaw said he and his wife had agreed it would be best for them if they gave up all formal ties with me and returned me to my sister's custody. He suggested I prepare to leave Siangi in the morning.

At first I was not able to speak, but then I tearfully begged Agaw to reconsider. I told him my return to Yamyamo would mean certain death. Mang José would be sure to track me down and kill me with his badil. Pensive for a long time, Agaw finally said, "I will think about this tonight and tell you my decision in the morning." He left me sitting there and went back into the house.

I was so immersed in my thoughts I did not notice Lando until he was standing next to me. He had a bundle of cogon for the roof of a hut he was building for himself. He eagerly accepted my offer to help him with the building. The only time Lando had married had been to a shrew, an experience that had made him a hard-rock bachelor.

Early the next morning Lando and I were in the ravine harvesting rattan for the hut. As we walked, Lando told me of his desire to someday attend the school in Batangas. Agaw was opposed to the idea. I learned that the school was exclusively for Buhids. Lando's enthusiasm for an education impressed me, and I planned to consider the idea for myself, later.

There was a profusion of rattan vines in the ravine, but getting to them posed a challenge. The sides of the ravine were almost vertical. Because of my light weight, I had the best chance of scaling one side of the ravine. I went up the side slowly until I came to a hanging vine. Reaching for it, I disturbed some pebbles, which rained on me. When I reached bottom, I found Lando waiting with his arms outstretched in case he had to catch me. We collected long vines which we tied to the hanging rattan, so that by swinging back and forth we were able to yank it loose at a good height from the ground. In this way we avoided being pelted with falling stones. At mianit mashohod mita we returned to Agaw's house with an impressive supply of rattan. Talking with Lando and Agaw that evening about our progress on the hut, I was relieved that Agaw did not mention his decision on whether or not to banish me.

Lando and I were alone on the fantao when Amit and Tinay joined us. Tinay was impressed with the excellent swimming holes in Siangi. She said that in Tauga they had only one main river for bathing and that was too deep and hazardous for swimming. The number of huge eels in that river kept even the most inquisitive children away. One of the great legends in Tauga is that a giant white eel is the queen of all the others, and she is white because she eats people.

In the middle of the night I had a visit from both Amit and Tinay. I was exhausted by morning.

Lando and I conquered the boredom of our work by having a song contest. It was long past noon when we arrived home to eat; we had become so engrossed in the singing contest we had not noticed the time. There were two men waiting to see me. One of them I recognized as Ganit (one of Amit's former husbands), but the other was a stranger. The stranger was introduced as Julio, son of Yaba of Elya, who had a message for me from my sister Tomay. This made me suspicious that Mang José was attempting to lure me back to Yamyamo. Tomay was actually my half-sister; she had not made any previous attempt to get in touch with me. I asked that they talk to Agaw. Afterwards, Agaw told me he was convinced Julio was a legitimate runner and his message was genuine, so I should prepare to leave immediately. The messenger explained that Tomay's oldest boy, Dagdagan, was critically ill, and Tomay wanted me to meet him before he died. They lived in Balingaso, which was two days distance from Elya.

Taking me aside, Agaw gave me a few pesos, and advised me to be very watchful while traveling. At the slightest suspicion that I might be drawn into a trap, I should return promptly to Siangi. Should I encounter serious difficulty, Agaw urged me to use his name. I said farewell to all present, and attempted to ignore their unhappy looks with a hearty assurance that I would be back soon. I was as doubtful of that promise as they were.

13 Government Is Integrity

We stayed at Anam's, near Siangi, the first night, because Julio wanted to ask him the best way to avoid Mang José. Anam was waiting for us. He had had Ganit show Julio where I was living.

Folo has sirang—5:00 A.M.—the next day we started our trip to Toman Malaglay, where we would stay with Linong. We stopped to eat lunch at a creek filled with shrimp—halayan. Julio was delighted, and caught twenty to my four. Although he helped me start a fire to cook mine, he preferred to eat his raw.

Julio was taller than any Buhid I had ever seen. He was silent at first, but as he grew comfortable with me he entertained me with fascinating stories about his work. In his travels to so many distant places, he learned to forage; he could not carry sufficient supplies. We discussed many topics, exchanged opinions, and compared our experiences. Julio gave me much wise advice.

After we reached Linong's, but before Julio could introduce me, his wife Omayan, embraced me. Such affection from a stranger baffled me until Linong told me that Omayan was my mother's sister, therefore my aunt. It was a joyous discovery: my own aunt. When Omayan told me how Enes nursed me after my mother died, I was pleased to tell them I had recently met Enes and her husband Do-ngay. I learned more about the history of my family that night than I had before. My mother had three brothers and four sisters, Omayan being the oldest. She told me my grandfather, Agwin, lived in Betolon, only a two-day walk from where we were, and suggested we go there so I could meet him. Omayan was not sure exactly where he lived but was certain someone in Betolon would know. Buhids transfer their homes as frequently as they do their kaingins.

A special breakfast of rice, broiled fish, and the luxury of coffee with sugar was ready when I rose at dawn.

As Julio and I set off on our trip, the sun was so hot we took full advantage of the shade of the forest. As we ate our lunch under a large tree, a pack of monkeys gathered about us and started chattering. Julio stood up, rushed to the trunk of the tree, and searched from branch to branch. When I asked him what he was looking for, Julio shushed me and placed his fingers over his lips to tell me to keep quiet. A bit later, he told me he was looking for a fanoyaw. I questioned him excitedly, especially when he said that unless we were extremely careful we might be killed.

Julio explained that whenever a group of monkeys assemble, particularly young ones, a large monkey is usually nearby to protect the smaller ones. The fanoyaw decides whether or not you mean to harm the young monkeys he is protecting. Once it determines that you are a threat the fanoyaw removes one of the points from its tail, and using its own tail as a bow shoots the point at you. Besides being very wise, it has a long tail with eight points at the end. A point fired by a fanoyaw never misses its target; it is impossible to elude it, even though you run in a circle or a zigzag. If we had given any sign we meant to harm the monkeys, the fanoyaw would have killed us while we were eating. That was why Julio had signaled me to be silent. I admired Julio for his bravery and for risking himself while serving as a messenger.

Although it was not yet evening when we reached the creek bordering Betolon, Julio decided we should stop for the night because it would be fatal if we passed the place of Farayfayon and the Fanlalatoy when it was dark. According to legend, a person named Farayfayon was responsible for the invasion of the Muslims against the Mangyans, and his lust for killing women was so great it turned him into a cannibal—fanlalatoy.

After surveying the area, Julio selected a high spot near the edge of the creek to camp. We gathered tree bark and stakes to build two afoyos. Finding a tree with the right bark, we peeled off two pieces to fit our heights; in another place we found the right size tree from which to make stakes, and the vines Julio wanted. Then he showed me how to set up an afoyo. He looped one end of the peeled bark to a straight branch, and sewed the top together. He then drove two stakes into the ground several feet away and attached the other end of the bark to them. Our afoyos were only knee-high from the ground. Julio then set about making the afoyos safe from danger. He secured branches from a habag tree, the only tree most snakes fear. Rashly, I suggested we should just sleep under a habag tree for maximum safety. In reply, Julio asked if I had ever heard of any Buhid sleeping inside a forest. It was the first time I had ever thought about it, but I had to admit I never had. He told me some frightening stories he had heard from the old folks about those foolish people who had slept in a forest.

Within the habag branches surrounding each of the afoyos, Julio arranged his arrows in line with them, so the arrowheads pointed alternately toward the afoyos and away from them. At the same time he recited a daniw, too fast for me to get the words. The incantation indicated that the arrows were intended to keep away evil spirits, such as the baboy gayat that usually roams at night. The baboy gayat makes a noise so much like a wild pig caught in a trap that many people go out to check. It catches them, and eats them alive. The evil spirit labang bayan sounds very much like a deer approaching, but turns into a giant cannibal. The one everybody had heard the most stories about was the evil spirit aswang, that looks like a man, but separates its body, the upper half flying during the night, foraging for human intestines. It usually changes into a bat to gain entrance through a window, and once inside returns to the shape of the upper portion of a human body, to prey on its victim.

Julio produced from his bayong two pieces of flint, which he called *santik magurang*, and started a fire with only two strikes of the stones. Two chunks of dried, salted pork were the next thing Julio took from his bag. Seeing me hesitate to eat the piece he offered, Julio assured me it was not wild pig.

Buhids believe that eating the dried, salted meat of a wild pig will diminish the chances of catching them. A Buhid must be naked when he eats the fresh meat of a wild pig, or he will never capture another.

It was a clear, cloudless night, but the fire felt good as we sat there listening to our pork cooking. Julio told me more about his experiences as a messenger. When he was still very young, his father began training him to be a runner. At the start Julio often cried with fear, but he learned to overcome it. A messenger, or runner, is called a *tagadia*. There are two different types of tagadias: some perform such duties as getting someone for family matters, as Julio did; the others, called *tagadia taga-ahon*, apprehend persons summoned by their chief to answer charges of violations of law.

This was all new to me, but I told Julio about having met a man who was carrying food to a family in distress, and I wondered if this sort of work was part of his duties. Julio explained that it is the tagadia fanganons who perform such relief work.

Although the tagadias receive no pay for their work, only the most responsible men are appointed by their chief. Julio's father was appointed, and trained Julio to help him. Because he was quite old, Yaba sent Julio on the long, arduous trips. Tagadias are invited to every poncion in the community, and some people present them with gifts of panaongens, in appreciation of their services.

Julio agreed that their political structure rested on the integrity of the tagadias. He said that if he had failed to locate me in Siangi and to bring me to my sister, she would probably lose her respect for the chief, and when enough people lose confidence in him, he is no longer effective. I did not like to admit that while I was in Siangi I had taken no notice of our political process in operation. Until Gamit had come with Julio in search of me, I did not know he had been appointed as a tagadia by Chief Agaw.

When I told Julio what I had learned about the tagadia system from the community mail censor in Opay, he explained that their system was different from the tagadia in his community. In Opay the tagadia merely delivered letters, whereas the tagadias from Julio's area had to accomplish certain missions; if they failed they lost their tagadia position and the high respect of everyone in the community. When a tagadia is entrusted to deliver money, he is bound to guard it with his life. He must pay a fine of double the amount of money he loses, and, to the mortification of his family, he is discharged.

Lying in my hammock, I thought deeply about the many things Julio had discussed with me. His profound regard for the welfare of his people made me feel ashamed. I began to appreciate what Agaw had tried to teach me about the obligations of leadership and community needs. Chief Agaw and Julio would judge my instability as lack of integrity. Both of them would choose death over the charge of neglecting their duty. These reflections started me thinking about my sister Tomay, burdened with grief over her dying son Dagdagan. I wished very hard that I might be able to do something for them.

We munched raw shrimp for breakfast as we walked. On our way we met a small boy fishing. Although he was familiar with most of the people living in that area, he could not tell us anything about my grandfather Agwin, since we could not give a description of him. An old man carrying a sack of corn told us Agwin lived beyond the three mountain ranges, North of where we were standing.

Julio showed surprise and remarked that the area was Bangon territory. He wondered what Agwin would be doing among those "tailed ones." Amazed, the man replied that Agwin was one of them, being half Buhid and half Bangon.

Bangons are believed to be wild, fierce, and only half human. It is extremely rare for a Buhid to mix with Bangons. When the old man asked why we wanted to see Agwin, Julio said I was Agwin's grandson, but because of the urgent need to get to my sister's, we could not take the time to travel the long distance to his house. Julio asked the man to tell Agwin I would see him on my return trip.

We hurried toward a fasongsongan Julio knew of to avoid what promised to be a heavy rain. Sitting under the fasongsongan with Julio, I eagerly quizzed him about the Bangons. I was curious to know if the Bangons did have tails. Julio could only say that he had heard the story many times. I had heard there were holes in the floors of Bangon houses for their tails to go through when they sat down. Julio had heard that story, too, and many more, but his personal experiences did not prove them, so he had decided the stories were told to discourage intermarriage.

We finally decided how the myth of the Bangons having tails started. Unlike the Buhids, who have learned to cultivate cotton and make their clothing, the Bangons wear a G-string made of tree bark. Since the Buhids rarely see them up close, the dangling bark fibers seen at a distance would look like tails.

The rain gave no indication of stopping so we decided to continue our trip. We picked leaves from an edick tree, one of the most common, and by weaving these together Julio made a piece of material big enough to cover our heads and backs, like a hood.

We realized the vine bridge would be washed away before we could possibly reach it. Our best chance of crossing the creek was to do it at the narrowest place we could find. To spare me from making the excuse that the current was too strong for me, Julio suggested we tie a long vine around our waists and he would go across first and then pull me across. The current was so strong I had to race along the bank to keep abreast of Julio, who was carried downstream. The place he started from was only fifteen arms' lengths across, but by the time he reached the other side we were at a spot where the banks were thirty arms' lengths apart. I needed Julio's help to keep going through that wild water. Finally I landed about ten arms' lengths downstream from Julio.

We were doing a running walk before I had stopped panting from my crossing. This, Julio explained, was to keep us warm and to make up for lost time. He had to shout to me because of the torrential rains. We kept up this trot for a surprisingly long time. When we came to a high mountain with a cave at the base, I urged Julio to take a short rest. As I was about to enter the cave, he held me back, saying he wanted to check it first. Julio examined the mountain, and refused to go into that cave because there were not enough trees to hold the soil and with the heavy rain we might be trapped by a landslide. He soon discovered another cave he thought much safer. Entering it, I fell flat, completely exhausted, shivering, and with my teeth chattering. I lay there a long time. The cave could not have held more than five people; the walls were hard stone, but it was dry and warm. We ate some half-cooked pork, and I took a brief nap before we continued.

The sun broke through as we came out. The river was brown from flooding silt, so I relied on the rain-filled leaves for drinking water.

Night fell just as we arrived at Yaba's house. I waited on the fantao while Julio gave his report to his father. Then they both joined me. Yaba was short compared to Julio, but it was evident why a chief would recognize in him a high sense of duty. His face was so serious as to appear stern, although he was most amiable. He told me the tagadia from Chief Yon-og had been waiting for me, but had to leave on another important duty, so Yaba himself would take me to Chief Yon-og, who would in turn take me personally to my sister's house. All that Yaba was able to tell me about my nephew's condition was that Dagdagan complained of such severe stomach pains that he could not eat and he had a high fever. Yaba calculated that Dagdagan had been sick for thirteen days and was close to death. We were to leave in the morning for the Chief's house.

I thanked Julio for the hardships he had endured on my behalf, as well as for the many lessons he had taught me about survival.

Yaba did not neglect my education either. He told me much about the customs of the West. I learned what an honor it was to have Yon-og, the Chief of the Beribis in the West, personally escort me to my sister. Yaba soon extracted from me my entire life's story. When Yaba discovered that the tree we sat under to eat our noon meal was full of honey bees, he decided to find the falafay. I quickly gathered up enough wood to start a fire. I had experience in smoking out bees from their hives. When Yaba gave me the hive, I took it down near the creek, and he went after bamboo cuttings to use as containers for the honey. We broke the hive into two sections, and after we took all the honey we wanted, we ate the raw eggs inside.

Upon being introduced to Chief Yon-og, I gave him the Beribi greeting my father had taught me. I raised my right hand to my ear with the palm opened, and made the slight bow which signified a greeting of profound respect. The Chief gave me the honor of sitting next to him. He had known my parents well, and asked why I had not visited my sister before. I told the Chief of my ordeal with Mang José. He was enraged, and if Yaba had not told him that Chief Agaw had specifically requested he be allowed to settle the matter, Yon-og would have had Mang José brought before him to answer charges.

The next morning Yon-og's wife told me her son Takip had

been sent to tell my sister I was coming. He had returned in the middle of the night and told them my nephew was still alive. It had been late, so Chief Yon-og had decided not to wake me.

14 Back to My Birth and My Mother's Grave

Recalling Yon-og's promise to tell me the full story of my mother's death, I asked his wife, Maniw, if she knew any of the details. Maniw said she knew only that a man named Badham had murdered my mother by slashing her neck. I was stupified. She could not furnish any further information, but she urged me to ask Yon-og because he was one of the first at the scene of the tragedy.

After breakfast, Yon-og and I set out on the final leg of my journey to Balingaso. I was particularly anxious to start because I was impatient to hear the details of my mother's tragic death.

Yon-og told me that a few days after my birth my mother had carried me with her to a neighbor's house to get a bayong of corn. On her way back home, she stopped at Badham's house to ask his daughter to sell her a chicken. The girl gave my mother a chicken, but refused any payment; she knew my mother had recently had a baby. It is a custom that the mother of a newly-born child should eat as much chicken as possible, but not from her own supply of poultry. Chickens must either be bought by her or be given to her.

While walking through some bushes on her way back home, my mother suddenly fell flat on her back, as if she had been pushed hard. A man named Canyogan happened to be walking directly behind her and saw that when she fell I was thrown into the bushes. I was crying loudly, but my mother picked me up before Canyogan reached her. Terror stricken, my mother rushed home without bothering to pick up the corn or the chicken. Canyogan tried to catch up with her to give her the chicken, but although my mother could not run, Canyogan could not reach her. He noticed another set of footprints beside my mother's, and he later swore they looked like hoofprints and that he also saw drops of blood. Being a fangamlang himself, Canyogan realized my mother had been attacked by a fagablang, so he followed her home.

Because my mother had last stopped at Badham's before being struck down, Canyogan concluded Badham was behind the attack. Badham was notorious for invoking the fagablang against others.

My mother was climbing the ladder to her house when she screamed in agony and fell to the ground, clutching her neck with her left hand; Canyogan was there almost in time to catch her.

Canyogan's shouts for help brought my sisters rushing out of the house. After handing me to Tomay, he carried her into the house by himself. Yon-og's brother Bawi heard Canyogan's shout, and discovered my mother's neck had been slashed by a fagablang. Canyogan sent Bawi to get Sulnay, because he was the foremost fangamlang in that area, and another man volunteered to notify Chief Yon-og.

Arriving there, Chief Yon-og found my mother writhing in pain and accusing Badham of her injury. She was talking as if Badham was there, and repeatedly tried to stand up and fight him. It took several men to restrain her. When she was able to recognize those around her, she turned to Chief Yon-og and accused Badham of setting the fagablang against her.

The two fangamlangs, after a long consultation, reported to Yon-og that her life could not be saved. Her wound, although invisible except to a fangamblang, was fatal. They were amazed that she was still alive and able to speak plainly.

It was dusk when my father and my mother's father, Agwin, arrived panting. My father rushed to her side, calling her name. They embraced, and he and my grandfather started crying. Tears rolled down my mother's cheeks as she said she knew she was dying and implored all those present not to bury her baby; she wanted her baby to live so her spirit could watch over it. When the crowd saw the fangamlangs shaking their heads, they left, concluding her final hour was near. My sister Mabanay prepared a fangobonan for my father to place on his wife's finger and another one for mother to place on my father's finger. The ring of panaongens, which is placed on the last finger of either hand of a dying wife or husband, is removed by the person who will carry the deceased to the grave.

Minutes after midnight my mother stood up again and angrily denounced Badham. It took three men to hold her down. She did not get up again. Canyogan told my father everything he had seen, and offered the opinion that Badham's daughter might have told her father that my mother had taken the chicken without the girl's permission, provoking Badham to seek revenge.

Mother, in a faint voice, asked father for her fangobonan, and when it was on her finger he placed the other ring in her palm, and she put it on his finger. The fangamlangs left with Chief Yon-og, leaving my father and grandfather alone with her. It was not long before the people waiting in the yard heard my father give a loud oliso, signaling the moment of death.

People began leaving the yard. As they did, they heard my father bellow for Banday, the Chief's deputy, to bring Badham there by sunrise. This meant trouble; Badham was famous for inflicting evil. There was much fear among those who came near the house at sunrise.

Badham arrived in the morning, seething over my mother's accusation. Several of those present tried to stop him from entering the gate, for they feared what might happen if he and my father met. Chief Yon-og asked Badham to calm down and return to his home. Badham's outrage made him deaf. He forced his way into the yard, in spite of the taboo forbidding anyone from entering the yard of the dead, and shouted that my father should apologize publicly for saying that he was responsible for my mother's death.

The air was heavy with tension. Accompanied by two of his deputies, and disregarding a serious taboo, Chief Yon-og entered the yard to prevent trouble. To everyone's astonishment, my father came out carrying my mother's body and flung it at Badham. The shock stunned Badham and knocked him to the ground, with my mother's body grotesquely sprawled across him. My father shouted to Badham to look at the murder he had committed. He ordered Badham to bring the body back into the house and wrap it in buri or, he threatened, Badham would be buried with her.

In his state of rage and grief my father was not even aware he had violated the taboo forbidding a body to be brought through a door; a wall of the house must be opened for bringing the body out.

The mob of spectators commanded Badham to comply. The house was only waist-high, so Badham removed a section of one wall, lifted the body up, and placed it inside the house. Everyone watched Badham enter the house to wrap the body in a mat. Badham asked my father why he insisted on charging him with murder. My father roared at Badham that the victim herself had repeatedly accused him, pointing out that both fangamlangs stated she had died from a wound inflicted in her neck by the fagablang, and that Badham frequently called upon the fagablang to do harm.

Badham protested his innocence, but my father challenged him to take the "lifting test." My father addressed his dead wife, telling her Badham was going to try to pick her up. He instructed the corpse that if Badham was not guilty she was to make herself light enough to be lifted by him, but if he was guilty she should make herself so heavy he would be unable to lift her the slightest distance from the floor. Then my father turned to Badham and ordered him to lift the body and thereby prove himself innocent.

An awesome silence gripped the people looking on.

Bending over, Badham put one arm under the neck and the other under the legs and proceeded to lift, but the body would not budge. He braced himself, bent his knees slightly, and with muscles in his neck protruding, tried once again, but it was as if the body was nailed to the floor. He could not lift it.

"Murderer! Murderer!" my father shouted as he ran over to a stack of spears in the corner of the room. Badham leapt out of the house, and one of the tagadia taga-ahons shielded him with his own body to prevent my father from spearing him. Agwin restrained my father and finally succeeded in taking his spear. Badham, looking like a trapped animal, remained in the yard, frightened by the menacing people outside the fence. Having seen conclusive evidence of his guilt, the crowd's murmuring turned into screams.

Coming out onto the fantao, my father shouted to Badham that he must carry Yaon's body to the burial place and dig the grave, or he could plan on being in the grave with her before sunset. His behavior betrayed my father's distress. He was again in conflict with sacred customs by demanding this of Badham. The nearest kin, or a witness at the death, is supposed to carry the body to the grave.

Before Badham could protest Chief Yon-og signaled that he had better do as my father demanded or no one there would be responsible for his safety.

At nopnoan sa gamat my father called for Badham to get the body and take it to the burial place. Entering the house, Badham whipped out his bolo and struck my father twice on the shoulder. Miraculously, my father was not hurt, but drew his bolo and slashed at Badham. But Badham sidestepped the blow, and my father's bolo went through the doorpost.

Chief Yon-og and two of his deputies stormed into the house, in time to separate the two men so the funeral services could continue.

My father had to open my mother's tightly closed fist, because we believe that if a dead person's fist is closed the body is holding its spirit in this world, and unless the fist is opened, the deceased person will continue to roam on this earth. He then undid her knotted hair, to allow it to air a short time before re-knotting it. This must be done to free the spirit of a living person which might be hiding in the tied hair. If the spirit of a living person is allowed to remain in the knotted hair of the dead, that person will die directly. The body was wrapped in a mat, and my father helped Badham lower it through the wall. Outside the house the body was prepared to be placed in a naoban. The arms and legs are folded so that the body can be put into the container in a sitting position.

Reluctantly, Badham carried the body. So many who attended the funeral were in an ugly mood, believing that Badham had caused the deaths of their own loved ones, they could hardly keep their hands off him. After Badham had finished digging the grave, the body was unwrapped, and my father recited the graveside daniw before he straightened the legs and went into the grave to have Badham lower the body to him. My father searched the body to make sure nothing had been removed.

The nearest relative of the deceased, before preparing the

body for burial, recites the daniw: "I am now going to place you in your resting place. Do not make yourself so stiff that I cannot straighten you out, or I will leave you outside for insects to eat you."

The cover was placed over the body, and my father placed all my mother's worldly possessions on top of it. Mabanay sang the farewell song, and then my father gathered up my mother's possessions: a bolo, a bayong, a pot, and a few other incidentals, to carry back to the bahay bahayan.

I was told that relatives took my baby hands and helped them place the first handful of dirt on my mother's grave. Tomay built a fire at one end of the grave to cook food, while the Chief and my grandfather built a miniature table on top of the grave. Each person at the funeral put the food he had brought for the occasion into the pot. This is usually bananas, small pieces of sweet potato, and gabi. When the "meal" was cooked, each contributor took a small portion and placed it on the table saying: "Take this as a humble offering, but we shall give a big poncion in your honor on the seventh day." Each then gave an offering of panaongens, followed by a gift of aromatic leaves to beautify my mother's spirit during its journey to the world beyond.

Then my father sang the following song over his wife's grave: "My beloved wife, how heavy is my heart that you have left me to live in this world of sorrow. I have loved you with all the love I can give, as you have loved me. And now, even though you have left me, I shall continue to love you and cherish your memory until the end of my life.

"Let your spirit guard over our beloved children who shall see you no more, but I shall guard them. Farewell but for now, my beloved wife, for we shall meet again in the Land of the Rising Sun. Farewell!"

My grandfather placed earthen pots at the foot of three trees growing near the grave, one for each of my dead sisters and one for my mother. Tomay placed two lighted sahings, one at the head of the grave and one at the foot. Many others scattered bamboo needles all over the grave, and two men placed bamboo thorns and sharpened sticks of bamboo about the grave to insure her safe passage to the Land of the Rising Sun.

There is a huge legendary snake that obstructs the path of the departing soul. The dead, therefore, are furnished with an ample supply of bamboo needles to blind the snake, so they can pass it safely.

Souls travel first to the East, where a legendary dog chases them to the West, which has rivers of fire. The bamboo thorns are provided to throw at the dog, stopping him. The next obstacle to reaching the Land of the Rising Sun is a plague of worms all over the body of the deceased which he scrapes off with the bamboo sticks. If he overcomes the dog and the worms, he will then encounter Mangaw, the cruel husband, and his wife Enabay, who with her daughter Daga offsets her husband's viciousness with kindness. If the deceased is a woman, Enabay meets her and gives her new clothing, urging her to change quickly lest Mangaw happen upon them first, and chase her toward the river of fire in the West. Deceased men are given a new G-string by Daga; they too are urged to change quickly, for the same reason.

While my father and grandfather marked the trees surrounding the grave to indicate a place of the dead to any who might otherwise set up a kaingin there, Badham and the Chief built a bonfire for everyone to jump over. It is believed that if one does not jump over the graveside fire, he goes home as cold as the dead, and his family will avoid him.

After the fire jump, the cortege of mourners is reversed, the last becoming the first on the homeward procession. When the funeral party reached my father's house, another fire was built for all to jump over. If one fails, he will be the next to die. As Badham was about to jump, my father shoved him into the fire, singeing his hair. My father demanded that Badham serve the seven days of quarantine with him and my grandfather, but Chief Yon-og refused, believing my father intended to kill him.

A great poncion was held on the seventh day after my mother's death, because, according to Chief Yon-og, she had loved and was in turn loved by many men. My father, Tipig, was her tenth husband.

And with the end of that enlightening story of my earliest history, we reached the little hill on which my sister's house stood.

15 A Long Visit With My Own People

Inside my sister's house a woman nursed twins, and in the opposite corner a man squatted close to a small boy who lay very still.

The boy had to be Dagdagan. My first impulse was to embrace my sister, but the Chief had told me not to say a word until he had introduced me. From their conversation I learned that Tomay had heard I was a fangamlang and had sent for me hoping I might be able to cure Dagdagan. My sister told Chief Yon-og that if I did not arrive by the next day they would place Dagdagan in Sulay.

Placing someone in Sulay is peculiar to the Beribi. If a person with a lingering illness shows no sign of recovery, he is placed in a small hut built for him in the forest. A fangamlang places food beside him while reciting daniws. The patient is told he must show a will to live by eating, and if he does not, he will be buried in two days. This threat is not actually carried out; relatives remain near the death hut, and occasionally one of them tries to tempt him to eat. If the person in Sulay makes an attempt to eat, he is returned to his home and treated with herbs. If he makes no attempt within the two-day period, the fangamlang drags a chicken around the death hut and recites an incantation. More food is placed next to the patient by the fangamlang, who repeats the threat to bury him if he refuses food.

For the next two days the relatives follow their previous sick-watch. If there is no response, the fangamlang, while reciting daniws, passes a squealing pig over the patient many times. The pig is tied to a tree for one hour then slaughtered. The fangamlang smears the patient's neck, chest, and stomach with the pig's blood, and a small piece of pork is cooked and offered to the patient. If he refuses this, he is left to die. He is checked periodically by relatives. After he dies, he is taken back to his home for a proper burial. If the patient in Sulay happens to be old and without relatives, he is left in the death hut to die and rot, or sometimes he is buried alive.

I was happy to hear Tomay tell Yon-og she had given birth to twins just a few days before. Moved by my sister's distress, Yon-og promised her I would arrive in time. Dramatically, he turned, saying to Tomay, "Meet your brother." Almost hysterical with delight, Tomay leapt to embrace me. We both cried from joy as we repeatedly kissed each other. She pretended anger at Yon-og for not telling her who I was. He replied that he wanted to be sure the trouble of bringing me had been justified. As Yon-og left, Tomay and I thanked him profusely for making our reunion possible. Chief Yon-og invited me to visit him.

I started checking on Dagdagan's condition. Though he was very weak he was able to understand what was said. When I asked him where he had pain, he placed my hand on his stomach. Tomay explained that he had been unable to keep food down and had refused food for several days. After an examination, with several incantations, I found Dagdagan suffered from a small fish he could not expel. A few days before he got sick, an old woman had asked him for some of the baglaws he had caught. He refused her. She was apparently a witch and had caused one of the fish to lodge in his stomach.

Dagdagan was perfectly cooperative. He drank the potions I gave him, and breathed deeply as I told him. I left him sleeping. Naay, the boy's father, sat stiffly next to Dagdagan as I worked on him. He displayed his first emotion when I asked Tomay to cook a chicken and make some broth. I had never seen such a transformation. Naay was older than he looked. Despite his forlorn appearance when I first met him, he was now actually handsome. He asked many questions about my potions. He insisted on preparing the broth himself.

Tomay had wanted to bury the twins at birth, but put it off so I could see them. Our father had told her never to keep twins because they always died, making the effort to raise them a waste. It surprised me to hear this from Tomay, because she was a twin to our brother, and both of them had lived. I argued with her to reconsider. She promised to discuss the matter with Naay again before making a decision.

Checking on Dagdagan, I was encouraged to learn that he was hungry. His parents were excited to see his improvement. In his desire to hasten his recovery, Naay offered his son a taya of soup and a cooked chicken leg. As tactfully as I could, I told Naay not to give so much at one time, rationing him only two tuways every two hours. I advised Dagdagan to sleep in between feedings. Naay impatiently waited for me to wake from a nap to report Dagdagan was begging for more food. I agreed to give Dagdagan the test to determine when a patient is ready to eat meat—the Baksonan. The patient is given a small piece of meat. As he bites it, if anyone sneezes or if the house lizard makes its love call, the patient is not ready for meat. Then, the Baksonan cannot be tried again for three hours.

We were all relieved when Dagdagan passed the test on the first try. No one had sneezed. He then took a taya of mashed sweet potato with broth and a half chicken leg.

With Dagdagan's recovery now certain, I told Tomay and Naay I dared not stay longer than one more day, for fear Mang José would learn of my presence. Tomay gave me cherished gifts from our father. One gift was a large blanket. Another was an unusual panaongen necklace, which was a special wedding gift of a male Beribi who married a non-Beribi. A rorum, a sanbong, and a broken bolo came as a set and would protect me should I unknowingly marry my sister. This was very wise of my father because my mother had had nine other husbands, and had born children he had never met. Our no-madic life and our casual marriages and divorces made it pos-sible for a married couple to discover they were actually brother and sister. It is believed that if the wife gives birth, the ground under their house will split wide open and a great geyser will engulf them and their home. The rorum, sanbong, and broken bolo are used to prevent this, in a ritual which must be performed at night by a special medicine man—a magdadaniw. First, he takes the rorum as he recites an incan-tation. Then he heats the sanbong until it is red hot, and thrusts it into the ground near one of the house posts while saying the proper incantations. He then heats the broken bolo until it is red hot, and sticks it in the ground next to the sanbong. When it cools, the magdadaniw strikes the bolo against a flint stone. If sparks are produced, he presents the stone to the couple.

A pig and a chicken are slaughtered and cooked. A portion

is given to the couple, and the balance is eaten by the magdadaniw and his helpers. The couple are then ordered to remain in their home for five days. They may talk to people, but they cannot take a bath, only wash their faces. On the fifth day the sanbong and the broken bolo are pulled from the ground and given to the couple. Another pig and chicken are killed, cooked, and eaten, with incantations. The couple can then remain married despite their blood relationship. The pigs and chickens used must be white, and a special type of tagadia, called *fanligao baboy,* finds white pigs and chickens for those ceremonies.

The famogad my father left me is a root of a particular tree. On a hunt, if you attach a small piece of famogad to your spear—right where the metal joins the wooden handle—good fortune in hunting is certain. However, for the famogad to act, contact with women must be avoided. There was also a salabay, a necklace made of plant twigs. When a hunter presents you with meat from an animal caught in the hunt, you must give him a piece of the salabay to insure him good fortune in future hunting.

The last gift Tomay had for me was the ceremonial marriage ax for males. I could not accept it in good conscience and insisted she keep it for Dagdagan. This ax offers a charm against a couple's separation if it is employed to cut down the first tree used to build their house. It also stops evil spirits from entering the house, providing the ax is used as a house post.

Tomay told me about my father's death. A neighbor, while out hunting, discovered my father in his small house extremely ill and alone. He ran all the way to Tomay's house to tell her. When they reached father's house, they found our sister Mabanay and her third husband, Waysag, with father. Waysag would have told me the news, but he feared Mang José. One of the tagadias tried to see me, but Mang José would not permit it.

Although a fangamlang was summoned, our father said he was eager to travel to the Land of the Rising Sun where mother was waiting. He wanted to last just five days more, so I might see him. Finally admitting that I would not arrive in time, father gave Tomay the things he wanted me to have. On the sixth day he said he could hear mother calling to him; he was anxious to be on his way. In his last words he deeply regretted allowing Mang José to take me away and hoped I would forgive him. He asked that I spend one day in quarantine for him, which I promised Tomay I would do, although I doubted I would ever have the money for a poncion afterwards.

I was startled when Dagdagan appeared beside me, asking for more to eat. I learned he was eight years old. Tomay amused me when she told me why he was named Dagdagan, which means "one who fell." When he was born, Dagdagan literally fell from the womb to the ground. Fortunately, their house was less than an arm's length above the ground.

Tomay told me Mabanay's babies were all stillborn, with dreadful deformities; one was without feet, another had no hands, but the most shocking was born with dog's ears. Although Mabanay had been asked to come during Dagdagan's recent crisis, she had sent word she could not come because she was heavy with a new baby.

When all of the children were asleep, I told Tomay and Naay about my recurring nightmare that Mang José was waiting for me on the trail with his badil. Naay told me he would take me to the Chief's by another trail. We agreed to leave early the next morning.

Once we were out of Mang José's range, I persuaded Naay to return. I reached the Chief's house by noon. Chief Yon-og cooked lunch, and invited me to stay for the night. Anxious to get back to Siangi, I declined and left shortly after the meal.

Yon-og's directions to Yaba's house were good, but trying to follow unfamiliar forest trails is difficult because they branch off frequently. I put markings on many trees in case I had to backtrack. I also asked people I met for their directions. I must have taken a wrong turn somewhere, because one person was amazed that I would try to reach Yaba's house that same day. A few people urged me to stop for the night. It was near sunset when I met an old man carrying a wild chicken. I asked if he knew anywhere I might sleep that night. He asked me where I came from and where I was headed. When I told him, he then asked my name. But I asked him to tell his name first, and his family status. His name was Gay-an. He told me all about his family voluntarily. Then he asked about me, as a formality, although he later told me he knew I had come from Siangi to cure Dagdagan.

According to our customs, when strangers meet, the first to request the other's name must permit himself to be cross-examined. When he has answered all questions satisfactorily, he can then ask questions. Had I refused to respond I could have been taken in for investigation—famgabaya—before the entire community or directly by the Hiyan Guragon, who had the arbitrary power to fine any amount. Noticing how late it was, Gay-an pointed out a house by the river, which he said was the home of one of his in-laws. He told me to tell the woman, named Naim, that I had talked with him, and he was sure I would be welcome for the night. Thanking him for his kindness, I left Gay-an with the vague feeling I knew the name Naim.

At the house was a boy a few years younger than I, named Rahoyan. He remembered me as a playmate. I used to play with him and his two older brothers, Dai-ionay and Agaw. Rahoyan's brothers were harvesting the kaingin with their mother. Their father, Gui-imnan, died a few months after mine.

When she returned from the kaingin and found me at the house, Naim gave me the warmest welcome I had ever received. Laughing and talking loudly about our wonderful past, I was startled by a sweet voice behind me, plaintively asking if I remembered her, too, from my childhood. Turning around I discovered a charming girl my own age, but I could not place her. After several seconds, Rahoyan shouted out, "Dadionay!" Memories of the little girl who played heroine in our games flooded back. Naim had to interrupt our pleasant recollections to ask for help in preparing the evening meal. Taking me out to the fantao, Naim asked me to tell her all about myself. She knew of Dagdagan's illness, and the fact that I had come to Balingaso from Siangi. She wanted to know how my visit had turned out. She told me to sleep in Dadionay's hut, since she was putting everyone working on the harvest in young Agaw's hut. Naim suffered from a severe cough, and had her children sleep in their own huts because her coughing disturbed everyone. She told me she and Gui-imnan had held Chief Agaw in such esteem they had named each of their children after a member of his family.

Later, in Dadionay's hut, and with Rahoyan, we started to exchange songs. I sang a love song in which I told Dadionay that the years which had separated us had not erased my yearning for her, and that life in its mysterious way had let us meet again. Dadionay blushed because she had to sing an answering song. She thanked the winds for blowing me her way, and lamented that those same winds selfishly sought to take me away from her. In answer, I sang how regrettable it was that the winds which blew the bird her way were so arbitrary, but if the bird in question could find a secure sanctuary no wind could ever carry it off again. The song warned that a hawk hovered nearby to swoop down upon the bird. Responding, Dadionay sang that there did exist such a sanctuary if the bird chose to take advantage of it, and she knew of no hawk near at hand.

Before falling asleep I decided to stay another day. Dadionay prepared breakfast for me while Rahoyan sought a bayong for me to use at the harvest. They did this while I slept. They guessed I would remain a few days.

On our way to the kaingin, which was three cigarettes away, I asked Dadionay how much of what a person picked was he permitted to keep. I intended to give my share to Tomay's family. The custom in that area was that each harvester kept everything he picked. Why, I asked Dadionay, did one own and maintain a kaingin if strangers reaped the harvest? Dadionay explained that the kaingin owner participates in his own harvest, which insures him and his family sufficient return to justify having a kaingin. Those who did not own kaingins were shy about always attending the harvests of others. So, it found a balance. Some were owners, some were itinerant pickers, but everybody had food. No one starved, and surplus food did not rot.

During the evening meal, a marriage proposal developed from my bantering, and I asked Naim's permission to "tie the free bird in the room." She responded, "The bird you seek to catch has enough feathers and is strong enough to fly away if it chooses not to be tied." Then Dadionay responded, "The bird may have full feathers and strong wings, but is it not also a fact the mother bird teaches its young how to use their wings before she permits them to soar freely into the sky?"

This exchange sealed my proposal of marriage. Naim welcomed me into her family because she always thought of me as one of her own sons. In deference to custom, however, she asked what I might offer as a dowry. I told her I had only one arm's length of panaongens. Naim accepted this and graciously added she would not have cared if I had only a dangao of panaongens.

To demonstrate her acceptance, Dadionay mixed her food with mine, and together we took a mouthful. Seeing this, Naim presented Dadionay with the traditional wedding mat, and young Agaw presented me with the wedding blanket.

"We'll have a poncion tonight!" he declared. He instructed Rahoyan and two other boys to catch three chickens and to start roasting them. Others were told to start pounding rice. More sahings were lighted. Most of the women did not wait to be assigned to a task. They went right to doing it.

Before the singing and merrymaking were ended, Dadionay and I retired to her hut, and Rahoyan thoughtfully found new sleeping quarters.

It was late the next afternoon before we wandered out to the kaingin. Naim was grateful for our help, because she would be able to start on Dadionay's kaingin in the morning. Harvesting that kaingin had a special significance for Rahoyan. As the youngest in the family he had not been allowed to work in any harvests since the death of his father, and Naim was going to let him help harvest in Dadionay's kaingin.

When either parent dies, custom prohibits the youngest child from helping in any harvests for a specified period, particularly if he is very young. The oldest children may eat nothing that has been freshly harvested for at least seven days, and they cannot work in any harvest during this period. Before the youngest member of a family can attend a harvest, he must undergo a test called *Pamahogan*. A hunter gives the child a piece of wild pig or deer meat. After the child eats, if the hunter's crops do not die it means the child has successfully passed the Pamahogan. This test can also be given to the child of a fisherman, using some of his catch. The child cannot eat the meat or poultry, or anything newly harvested, or even go near any newly planted crops until he has passed this test.

My future looked promising for the first time. I truly was happily married; I yearned to settle down with Dadionay for the rest of my life. We were discussing the building of our home when Dadionay noticed a friend of hers approaching at a run.

When he was able to speak coherently, Ragkop told me that Mang José had heard of my presence, and he was pursuing me at that very moment. My perpetual fear of that man tensed every fiber of my body. It killed my dreams of a settled life which had been so alive just a few minutes before. Fighting my instinct to flee, I asked Dadionay if she would come with me to Siangi. She wanted to talk to her mother first. A family conference was called. Young Agaw, unlike his namesake, wanted to stand fast and muster the aid of neighbors to fight off Mang José. I commended Agaw for his brave suggestion, but reminded him that Mang José carried a badil and could kill us all. Naim rejected my suggestion to take Dadionay to Siangi, because custom required that I would also have to take Naim and Rahoyan along with us. Since Naim could not leave, Dadionay would have to remain if I decided to go to Siangi. Dadionay and I both appealed to Naim to reconsider, but she would not.

Saying farewell to Dadionay, I promised to return to her, and Naim reminded me that Dadionay would be legally separated if I did not return in a month's time.

Late that evening I reached Yaba's house, and was delighted to see Julio again. Yaba was out cutting bamboo for benches for a poncion they were giving in a week, to honor a dead son. I remembered a friend who lived there in Elya. Both Julio and his mother knew my friend, Dangin, but knew him best by his nickname, Bonein, which is given to those who have the very common skin disease called *boni*. Julio kindly took me to Dangin's house. Surprised and happy to see me, Dangin insisted I stay at his house for the night. I consented to his wishes, and I told Julio I would see his father in the morning. Alone, I asked Dangin about his wife, Pokpok. She was a flirt, and a man named Boknol had lured her away from Dangin. He went on so about how generous Pokpok was with her favors that he soon convinced me to visit Pokpok with him, since her husband was away.

During the visit, with darkness coming, I made several signals to Dangin that I wanted to leave, but he ignored me and jokingly suggested I stay with Pokpok that night. My surprise at Dangin's hint turned to astonishment when Pokpok impudently invited me to stay with her. She even assured me I had nothing to fear from her husband; he had surprised her many times with other men. Before I could answer, Dangin excused himself, saying he would be right back.

Pokpok told me she still loved Dangin and therefore her present husband hated him. She had left Dangin because he had refused to be cured of his skin disease.

Dangin did not return, and I stayed with Pokpok. It was quite late when she came to my mat. At our most intimate moment, the door crashed open. A man appeared waving a lit sahing and screaming that he would kill me. It was obvious that he thought I was Dangin. I fled when I heard a bolo being unsheathed. As fast as I ran, I could hear Boknol close behind me, yelling his threats. At the same time Pokpok was screaming for Boknol to come back.

This tumultuous scene aroused many of the neighbors. Lit sahings from several directions seemed to converge on Boknol's house. I recognized Yaba carrying a sahing. Seeing me in obvious flight, he asked me what all the commotion was about. I was telling him the story when Boknol came upon us with his bolo in his hand and murder in his eyes. Yaba ordered Boknol to sheathe his weapon and quiet down, and told us to follow him to his house.

Boknol's story and mine agreed, so Yaba ordered me and Pokpok to each pay a fine of one arm's length of panaongens to Boknol. Yaba then fined Boknol one G-string to be paid to me, and one abul to be paid to Pokpok, because of the embarrassment he had caused by bringing so much public attention to a private affair.

Had Pokpok or I committed suicide as a result of our humiliation, Boknol would have been fined severely. Frequently, an adulterous wife or her lover commit suicide because of the shame of exposure. The proper way for a husband to deal with such a situation is to wait until the assignation is finished and then calmly arrange the fines to be imposed, thus eliminating any public embarassment.

Yaba reproached me for my lack of discretion, and counseled against doing anything so mindless in the future. I apologized for any embarrassment I had caused him, and thanked him for helping me. One more painfully acquired lesson was added to my education. I recalled that Chief Agaw had tried many, many times to teach me the same lesson.

Eager to be under way from Elya, I set off early in the morning, and by sunset I reached the settlement of Balwayan.

16 Love, Rape, and Murder All on a Sunny Afternoon

I entered the first house I came to, and with typical Buhid hospitality the lady of the house, Gaymay, welcomed me for the night. Her husband's name was Man-ed, and they had recently had a baby. Her two children by her former husband were my age, and her daughter, Aymay, caught my interest.

During supper I entertained the family with my recent adventures. Aymay listened closely. She plied me with questions about the world beyond their village of Balwayan, which she had never seen.

About midnight I awoke to discover Aymay pressed beside me, pinning me against the wall. Because of her innocent friendliness and my recent misfortune in Elya I would not take advantage of the situation.

At breakfast Gaymay surprised me with an invitation to stay another day, enthusiastically seconded by the whole family. Her son Ayon asked me to help him gather honey, but Gaymay asked us to stay with Aymay and the baby. Gaymay and Man-ed were going to their kaingin to pick a special bunch of bananas for their "guest of honor."

An hour after his mother left, Ayon asked Aymay if she would mind if we left just long enough to gather honey for the noon meal. She assured us she would be all right. We had not reached the forest when we heard a girl's screams for help and the loud cries of a baby.

"That's Aymay's voice!" Ayon shouted. We raced back to the house. We could see a man dragging Aymay out of the

107

house by her hair. Then he hit her twice on the head with a club. She stopped screaming. We started shouting, hoping to attract someone to help us. Hearing us, the man dropped Aymay, yelled to a friend, and the two of them ran away.

My first glance at Aymay's bleeding head told me she was critically wounded. I persuaded Ayon to sound an alarm instead of chasing the attackers, reminding him Aymay's injury should be our first concern. Using a bamboo piece specially designed for giving a distress signal, Ayon soon had a number of people rushing to our aid. I tore off Aymay's baruka to bandage the wound over her right ear.

The many people who gathered were shocked at Aymay's injury, and started arguing whether or not to take her into the house before her parents got there. As they argued, Gaymay and Man-ed arrived. Gaymay was hysterical, sobbing, kissing her daughter, and asking questions. Aymay was unconscious. Ayon and I could give only the sketchiest description of what had happened.

Quickly Gaymay took command of herself and the situation. She decided to leave Aymay on the ground until we could stop her bleeding. From her bayong Gaymay drew a white cloth which seemed to be an heirloom, and wrapping this around Aymay's head, she recited a daniw. She then made signs on Aymay's forehead. All I could understand from her daniw was that she was calling Aymay's spirit to return until her daughter could tell us what had happened, so the men involved could be punished. I learned that Gaymay could summon the spirits of those newly dead, but only to get information.

Despite what I learned, I was astounded when Aymay became conscious, as if she were awakening from a deep sleep. When she tried to get up, I held her down, explaining that she was seriously injured. She closed her eyes, writhing in pain as she felt her wound. Then she looked at me and her mother and finally at all the others as if asking why they were there. Ayon told his sister what we had witnessed, and asked if she could identify her assailants. Aymay said that immediately after we had left two men she knew as Bongak and Hombos came into the house. Hombos asked where Gaymay hid her pot of panaongens, and started searching. Bongak hugged Aymay. When she pushed him away, he threw her down and raped her.

Frightened by her screams, Bongak released her and she fled. He caught her on the ladder, grabbing her hair, and the last thing Aymay could remember was being clubbed.

The crowd shouted, "Bongak must die!" Ayon swore to kill Bongak. Gaymay asked everyone to be calm and help carry Aymay into the house.

When we laid her gently down, Aymay gripped my hand tightly, so I sat down beside her, and she smiled at me sweetly.

I could hear Gaymay whispering to her husband to get certain roots and the bark of certain trees which I knew were used to stop bleeding. Gaymay asked that not too many people come inside, fearing the house would collapse.

Aymay asked her mother to use her powers to stop her from dying at night. We believe the spirit will not be able to find its way to the Land of the Rising Sun if one dies in late afternoon or at night.

Aymay was not deceived by my assurances she would recover. It was a marvel she had survived so long. She thanked me for what I was trying to do, and confided she had intended to ask permission to go with me to Siangi. She whispered that she loved me.

I kissed her gently to express my love. Aymay pledged her love and promised to wait for my arrival in the Land of the Rising Sun. Holding my head with trembling hands, she pressed her face to mine.

Aymay held my hand tightly, even when she became delirious late that afternoon. Ayon, Gaymay, Man-ed, and two relatives kept watch with me throughout the night. The roosters' crowing wakened me, and Aymay was still holding my hand. Gaymay paced the floor murmuring daniws, and Ayon sat next to his sister. Neither of them had slept.

Gaymay told me I was the first boy for whom Aymay had ever expressed love. Seeing her interest, Gaymay was going to ask me to stay a little longer. She started crying so hard she could no longer talk.

Her mother's crying aroused Aymay. Her eyes were clear of pain. Squeezing my hand, she asked if I still loved her. I could only squeeze her hand, nod my head, and weep.

She said she could die happily because she had found a boy

who truly loved her. I kissed her to show how deeply I cared. She thanked her mother for bringing her safely through the night, insuring her a glorious journey to the Land of the Rising Sun. Aymay implored Ayon not to cry for her, as she was about to see their father and tell him what an excellent brother he had been. Ayon cried more loudly.

Aymay released my hand, begging me to stay for her funeral. She asked me to fix her hair. I unwound her long, bloodsoaked hair, combed it as carefully as I could, and knotted it in back. When I told her I was leaving her my comb, she guided my hand to stick it in her hair. She then told her mother to remove the bandage as she was now ready to leave us. I begged Gaymay not to, because once it was removed Aymay would die. Aymay told me she had to do it for her family's sake. Together Gaymay and I unwound the band as carefully as we could. When we finished Aymay urged me to go away from the house, because she could feel the spirit leaving her body.

The Buhids believe certain people have the power to give back life or prolong the life of a dying person. Gaymay knew that if she saved Aymay's life with this gift, a curse of violent deaths would plague her family for many generations. Knowing this, Aymay was resigned to death. The whole family believed they were cursed to die violently. Aymay's father had been killed by a spear when he tripped over a wild-pig trap.

Ayon pulled me out of the house. We had hardly reached the ground when I heard Gaymay's loud oliso, the official signal of death.

A special burial ceremony was needed for Aymay. A person who dies violently is considered totally unprepared for his trip and future life in the Land of the Rising Sun, and elaborate preparations are required at the grave site. At Gaymay's request, I removed the light cotton shirt I wore and placed it on Aymay's chest, so she could take the warmth of my embrace with her. Three strands of panaongens, one white, one black, and one red, were placed across her forehead. Many combs (which had to be wooden) were put in her hair by friends. Fragrant flowers of specified color were also placed in her hair. Strings of beads were placed across her chest and brass bracelets put on her wrists. To put on the bracelets,

Aymay's hands had to be forced open. Everyone chanted a plea to her not to be so rigid, and rigor mortis was not evident for the few minutes needed. Two skirts were also put on her body and a belt with bells attached. The belt was meant to keep Aymay happy by distracting her from any thoughts of the violence she had suffered in this world. Gay tin ornaments donated by the elders were placed on her feet. The oldest man in the village placed a large earthen jar before Aymay's body, which was in a sitting position. Everyone put strings of panaongens into the jar until it was almost full. Aymay was then placed in a reclining position, and her relatives straightened her legs. After wrapping the body in a mat, they lowered her into her grave. While the body was lowered, brass gongs were struck, another ritual for those who had died violently.

After the lunch which followed the funeral, I sadly said farewell. Gaymay hugged me and said she considered me her son-in-law. She realized Aymay and I had pledged our love to eternity.

---

17 Bright Beads Pay for Bad Deeds

By mianit kalimbaba I could see the familiar mountain ranges of Siangi. It would be well past sunset before I could reach Agaw's house. I decided to go to Anam's house for the night.

Three girls came to Anam's that evening to borrow litlit, but it was obvious they were interested in "catching a chicken." Immediately after supper Anam retired with his two wives and left Ganit, his helper, and me to entertain the girls. I caught all three, and at least two of them fluttered over to Ganit during the night.

Lohena was home alone when I reached Agaw's, and she told me everything that had occurred while I was away. Amit was married again to a man from Opay named Ayan, despite Agaw's objections. Neither of them had paid the necessary fines, so they were hiding out in the mountains because Agaw was so angry.

I saw Lando's completed house, of which he was justly proud; he had finished it by himself. I saw Agaw, Yonay, and Lando coming from their kaingin. Their greetings were exceptionally cheerful, or perhaps it just seemed so after my previous homecomings.

I screwed up enough courage to tell Agaw about my escapade with Pokpok. He was very upset because I not only might have been killed, but could have brought great trouble to others. Had Boknol killed me when I was with his wife, under Buhid law he would have had to pay a heavy fine to my wife (had I been married) and to all of my blood relatives who might submit a claim. Had Boknol killed Pokpok, he would have had to pay fines to her blood relatives. If Boknol had refused, or could not pay those fines, any of the claimants would have had the right to collect in kind: Boknol's life. If I had not been able to pay the fine imposed by Yaba, Boknol would have had the right to have an affair with my wife. I would have to tell my wife, and ask her to allow Boknol into her bed. Should my wife refuse, Boknol would have been entitled to request the same from my brother's wife. Should my sister-in-law refuse, I would be bound to ask my daughter to sleep with Boknol or his son.

If my wife consented, their rendezvous would be arranged so I would "happen" on them and thus suffer the same hurt Boknol had experienced.

Agaw was so carried away, he warned Lando of the pitfalls of my immoral conduct. Lando, now a confirmed bachelor, remained silent. Obviously, Agaw aimed his lecture on morality at Lando because I would not listen.

To divert Agaw, I told him of Aymay's tragic death. Although he was deeply sorrowful, he told me if she had lived, he would have had to object to our marriage because we were distant relatives. The Buhids do not allow marriage, or even sexual relationships, between relatives.

Once we were alone, I told Lando all the details I had not told Agaw about my latest travels. I never kept secrets from Lando, and I needed his help for what I planned to do. When I told him that of the three girls I had caught at Anam's the one who appealed to me was Pandak, Lando's eyes widened. He was upset that Pandak had agreed to marry me because she

Lando writing a letter on a piece of bamboo.

had already promised herself to Agni-pan, the brother of my former wife's lover, Ehit. To complicate matters further, Pandak's father, Ang-gin, and Chief Agaw were enemies. Lando did not believe Agaw would ever agree to our marriage. Lando did agree, however, to cover up for me to Agaw while I visited Pandak.

I moved into Lando's house, and at breakfast the next morning he told Agaw I would help him check his traps for wild chickens. Once we were out of sight, Lando and I separated. I headed for Anam's house. Shortly Pandak appeared. She pretended surprise at seeing me and told Ganit she had come to borrow some chewing tobacco for her father, the one request which made him leave us alone. He had to go outside and to

113

the back of the house where the tobacco leaves hung to dry. Pandak handed me a piece of inscribed bamboo, telling me to read it on my way home. Her message was in my bayong before Ganit returned. She thanked Ganit and left. He was baffled to learn that we had not taken advantage of his absence.

Pandak's message asked me to meet her at mianit kalimbaba in her cotton field. I made it a point to pass her house on my way to Lando's. Seeing her on the fantao, I acknowledged her message with a slight nod and a wink. She answered with a bewitching smile.

I hid in thick bushes at the appointed spot and was able to see anyone who approached. I soon saw Pandak and revealed myself. She signaled me to follow her to her hut. She asked if I was alone. Then, being assured I was, she insisted that we roast some corn, despite the attention a fire might draw.

Pandak was very proud of having many suitors. She asked if I was serious about my proposal, and when I said yes, she told me she loved Agni-pan and I would have to share her with him if I married her. The thought of the number of fines involved was discouraging. Pandak did not wait for my reply, but invited me to her parents' house three days later if I agreed to her conditions. She had already sent a letter to Agni-pan telling him to be there.

Pandak was not being frivolous. Serious thinking was required. While we allow polygamy, the conditions are so costly the practice is rare. First, fines must be paid to each of the three sets of parents, the amount to be determined by the recipients. The poncion which is mandatory for such a marriage is a community affair, held either where the three partners reside or where they plan to live. This poncion goes on for as long as the guests wish and usually lasts several days, requiring the slaughter of a dozen pigs and numberless chickens. Although these affairs are very expensive, if they fall short of the community's expectations, the three marriage partners are ostracized.

The vows of a polygamous marriage are: The bride must accept both men equally and must fulfill her wifely duties to each; each of the men must agree to share one wife and share equal responsibility; and all offspring must be claimed by both husbands. It was quite late when I left Pandak. She would not reconsider, because she loved us both.

As we talked late into the night about Pandak's proposal, Lando advised that I "forget that bird in the thorny bush and recatch Amit instead."

I was in a stupor for the next three days. Lando refused my invitation to go with me to the meeting. I knew he was afraid of offending Agaw by involving himself in my crazy adventures.

As I approached Pandak's parents' house, Agni-pan stopped me to say he had been courting Pandak for a long time. He accused me of deliberately coming between them. I retorted that if I could be guilty of such an act I had learned it from his younger brother, Ehit, who had traveled with Emian and me from Apnagan to Siangi for that express purpose.

Pandak's father, Ang-gin, noticed how passionate the arguing had become, so he invited us in, where we sat in opposite corners. When he learned we were both there seeking his daughter in marriage, Ang-gin asked Pandak to explain. She just sat there glancing from one to the other. Ang-gin said she must have rejected us both. I suspected he was trying to force her to name one of us. Pandak begged her father to give her time before answering, and he readily agreed.

When she entered the house, Yaay-nan, Pandak's mother, was followed by a crowd of neighbors who obviously wished to see the man fatahoyan. Their remarks about Agni-pan and me were unnerving. The contest was formally opened when Ang-gin demanded that the spectators be quiet so he could hear the two maman-tohoyans' statements.

Ang-gin asked us to repeat to his wife the proposals we had made earlier. Then Pandak was asked to reply. She bowed her head and remained silent for several minutes. Thinking she was unable to decide between us, many spectators started prompting her with hints of their choice. This started out as whispers, but swiftly grew into a roar of laughter and cheering. The scene lost any semblance of a staid family affair and took on the appearance of a cockfight, with opposite sides cheering wildly for their favorite.

Picking up a piece of bamboo, Pandak inscribed a message on it, and handed it to her father. Because Ang-gin could not read, he handed it to me, and Pandak requested I read it aloud. Addressed to her parents, it said Pandak decided to write because she was too embarrassed to speak. She loved Agni-pan and me equally, so she had decided to ask their permission to marry both of us.

Everyone was shocked. The house became silent. Ang-gin was the first to speak, refusing permission. Yaay-nan asked Pandak loudly if she had made any promises to either of us. Agni-pan shouted that he would not have traveled the great distance from Apnagan if he had not had Pandak's assurances of her love in both deeds and words. I stated I was prepared to make the same claim. Pandak fled from the house in tears.

Ang-gin asked us to repeat our claims, and then summoned Pandak. With red eyes, Pandak told the crowd she intended to stand by her decision. She would leave it up to Agni-pan and me. Ang-gin declared that neither he nor his wife approved, but Pandak was old enough to decide for herself, and they would resign themselves to her decision. Ang-gin then asked Agni-pan and me if we were agreeable.

While all the commotion was going on, I had been thinking seriously about the situation and had decided to withdraw. My strategy required that I gamble on the possibility that Agni-pan would not withdraw. If he withdrew, I would be burdened with many fines to pay: fan-ngagawan—three arms' lengths of panaongens—for having taken the girl from another; faniningonan—two arms' lengths—for having won the girl; familibana—two arms' lengths—to induce Agni-pan to forget his loss; and finally familibang hasadi hasadi—two arms' lengths—because my presence caused trouble between the other man and the girl. Pandak would also have to pay a fine, fumisilague—three arms' lengths of panaongens—for giving the losing suitor false hopes. Agni-pan would, in turn, be obliged to pay me one arm's length as a victor's reward.

Before Agni-pan could speak, I stated I could not accept the proposition. I demanded instead that Pandak accept just one of us and asserted I should be the one because of the promises she had made to me. Agni-pan declared he was opposed to the idea of sharing Pandak, and demanded she select him. At Ang-gin's urging Agni-pan and I went outside to see if we might settle the matter between us.

Agni-pan was more agreeable than I thought he would be When I stated I planned to withdraw so he could have Pandak, Agni-pan said he would also withdraw.

Back inside, I told Pandak and her parents I had decided to withdraw. In his brusque fashion, Agni-pan blurted that he was also withdrawing his marriage proposal. Pandak ran out of the house crying. Ang-gin made no attempt to hide his relief, but the spectators were disappointed.

Ang-gin was so impressed with our maturity, despite our youth, that he decided to pay Pandak's fines for her. Agni-pan and I each received one depa of panaongens. It was almost sundown, so Ang-gin urged everyone to go home.

If Pandak had decided to pick just one of us, the fine to the selected suitor would have been much less than it was when we withdrew. But since Agni-pan and I had both claimed she had promised to marry us, Pandak would have had to pay a stiff fine to the one she rejected.

---

18 Fana Fofos Are Lawyers—We Need Three

To be working again on Lando's kaingin was a relief. Chief Agaw was pleased that I was so productive. He hinted I should establish my own kaingin, and strongly implied that if I could be as amorous about working as I was about every girl I met I would soon have stability, the one quality Chief Agaw esteemed above all others.

About a month after the man fatahoyan, I visited Ano, Pandak's cousin, to borrow some mascada. Ano was curious about why I had withdrawn my proposal to her and we talked a long time. When I was leaving, I saw Pandak approaching. She gave me a cheerless smile and our conversation was at first guarded, but gradually we warmed to each other and Ano told us to come into the house.

Ano was a merry soul, and his amusing stories soon put Pandak in the mood to sing. She first sang about still wanting the comfort of my arms even though I had hurt her much. In song I asked her metaphorically why she insisted on marrying

117

two boys when she claimed to love one so deeply. Her sung answer was a vague defense of her actions. When we finished, I understood that if I was still interested in marrying Pandak, she was certainly interested.

With only a G-string to protect me from the chilly night air, I asked Ano for a blanket. He impishly suggested I seek the warmth I desired from Pandak, indicating that his wife was giving her a blanket. The spot Bayahat picked as Pandak's sleeping place was only one arm's length away from mine. The cold air and Ano's urging soon had me under her blanket. We decided to see her father the next day to ask his permission to marry. The following morning, Ano and Bayahat were elated at the news.

We were fortunate to find Ang-gin home alone with his wife, Yaay-nan. Ang-gin coldly asked what I wanted this time. Pandak bluntly asked for his approval of our marriage. She would have been wise to leave it at that, but she started explaining her motives for marrying me. Her explanation was as bewildering to me as it must have been to her father. She begged him to consent, even if our marriage lasted only a single day. Her main thought was that the community should know we were officially married, so she would have some claim on me.

His daughter's vulgarity upset Ang-gin. He asked if I was agreeable to the grounds she had cited. If I had agreed with him, I would have been questioning Pandak's judgment, which would only undermine our request. If I agreed with her, Ang-gin would think me a simpleton. I told him I agreed to her conditions. His disapproval, endorsed by Yaay-nan, required that I pay them a fine of one arm's length of pan-aongens.

Ang-gin started complaining to his wife about the younger generation, their selfishness, and lack of love for their parents. He believed the laws should be more stringent. Yaay-nan reminded him that he had refused to help her discipline their children; thus the fault for his daughter's actions was solely his.

Not surprisingly, Lando predicted unhappy results from the marriage when I told him the next day. I worked with him in the kaingin most of the day, and when I left I asked him to tell Agaw of my marriage.

To win my in-law's approval I lied, saying that I owned part of Lando's kaingin. They preferred Agni-pan as a son-in-law. He was from a wealthy family; I had little more than the G-string I wore and was the adopted son of Ang-gin's enemy.

Returning from Lando's kaingin a few days after I was married, I was surprised to find Agni-pan and several neighbors talking to Pandak and her father. Agni-pan accused me of being false to him by marrying Pandak. I could not convince him that Pandak had asked me to marry her after we had withdrawn our proposals. When all my appeals to reason failed, I finally offered to give him Pandak. Instead of being pleased, he became angrier. He refused Pandak, claiming I had scorned him, and demanded I pay him a fine. When it became evident that we were stalemated, Ang-gin ordered that each of us must be represented by a fana fofo—one who has developed the skill to argue another's cause in any dispute. So this matter could be permanently settled, the arguments would be heard by a balitangan taw. Serving as either a fana fofo or as the judge is a civic duty for which there is no payment. The cost of a poncion—the usual fine imposed—must be paid by the fana fofo who loses. Customarily, the principals of the dispute help the losing fana fofo pay the costs.

Pandak beckoned to a tiny old lady whom she called Aching. Agni-pan called on a middle-aged plump man named Wag-hag. My hopes of winning took off like monkeys to the trees, because Wag-hag had been my first choice. He was well known as a good fana fofo, even beyond Siangi. There was no one else in the group I considered as good. I was about to ask for a postponement when cheering started outside. Edium came through the door, and I almost screamed with delight. Not only was he a superb fana fofo with a wide-spread reputation, but he took delight in matching wits with Wag-hag. I announced Edium was my choice. A loud cry of approval greeted my statement. Ang-gin excused himself to find a balitangan taw. He returned shortly with Foy-foy, who was widely known for his fairness and wisdom. While we waited for Ang-gin, Edium coached me on what to say when I was called on to explain my side. Agni-pan was the complainant, so Pandak and I were the respondents.

Entering the house, Foy-foy demanded silence and then

119

called on Agni-pan to state his case. Agni-pan repeated his complaints and demanded I be ordered to pay him a fine for the injury I had done him.

When called to give my defense, I declared I was not there to defend my actions since I was not guilty. I protested the harm done me by Agni-pan in trying to disrupt my happy marriage to Pandak, which was lawful. Agni-pan shouted that I was twisting the facts. Declaring that Pandak and he had in fact committed themselves to each other long before I arrived on the scene, he argued that he had spent much to win her love and wanted payment for that and for the injury done to him.

I argued that if it were agreed that Agni-pan's claims were true, it did not make sense to pay his wooing expenses, since he had withdrawn his proposal voluntarily. I attacked his next argument, that he had withdrawn because of our mutual agreement, by reminding him I was the first to withdraw. Edium approved my argument with a generous smile. When I stated I had offered to surrender Pandak to Agni-pan if she would accept him, Aching, Pandak's fana fofo, interrupted to ask the balitangan taw if her client could testify to her feelings.

Though nervous, Pandak had been briefed by her fana fofo and spoke clearly. Pandak stated she had loved each of us, but when she wanted to marry both of us we withdrew. She did not know if our decision to withdraw was mutual. She believed, however, that when we withdrew she was no longer bound by any agreement to either of us. She had met me a few days after our withdrawals and had felt free to discuss marriage with me. Cheers rang out for her.

Agni-pan leaped up screaming that Pandak had lied. As he saw it, she gave her word to him before she ever met me. Pandak stated frankly that I was the first to propose to her. Noisy whispers rippled through the crowd; Wag-hag looked upset. After calling everyone to order, Foy-foy told the three of us to remove ourselves a good distance from the house. As we were leaving, he called the three fana fofos before him to present their arguments. He also told the audience he did not want to hear any comments.

We went in separate directions. I avoided talking to Pandak lest Agni-pan think we were conspiring against him. Agni-pan's face was a study; I could not help feeling sorry for him. I was so moved, I decided to see if we might not be reconciled. He was responsive to my friendly approach. Pandak soon joined us. She won us over by confessing she had lied about giving her love to me first, and apologized to both of us.

In the widening shadows of sunset, a man approached rapidly. It was Agni-pan's father, Malay-ay. I had not seen him since I had worked on his harvest with Emian and Eg-hay. Malay-ay reproached Agni-pan for having started a dispute court. He angrily explained to his son that had I been guilty of alienation it would have canceled their family's debt, owed because Ehit had separated Emian and me. Malay-ay ordered Agni-pan to go with him into the house to settle the matter. Pandak and I followed them.

All the loud arguing stopped when Malay-ay entered. Ang-gin ran over to greet him. They warmly embraced, and Ang-gin apologetically told his old friend that the children had gotten themselves into trouble and were straightening the thing out, and that Foy-foy was about to make a decision. Foy-foy commented that Malay-ay was more experienced as a ba-litangan taw than anyone he knew and asked if he might have any suggestions for solving the dispute.

Malay-ay said he had only the dubious account of his son and had come to get the truth. He was confident Foy-foy would give a just decision. Ang-gin's opinion was that the fault rested with his daughter's greediness to have two husbands. I was so moved I confessed that Agni-pan was the first to court Pandak and the first to be accepted. Foy-foy asked my fana fofo why I had come between Pandak and Agni-pan if I knew of their commitment. He reminded Edium that it was a finable offense to disrupt an engagement. Edium answered that I had my own reasons, which Malay-ay knew. Malay-ay conceded I had ample reasons.

Foy-foy asked if any of the three fana fofos had anything to add, but it was apparent they were puzzled, so he announced the fine of one pig from each fana fofo, to be served in the evening. The case was officially closed. There was loud applause from all but the fana fofos, whose faces indicated they would like to appeal to higher authority, which was impossible.

The poncion was well underway when I decided to go to bed. I could not find Pandak anywhere. Reaching the hut I was surprised to discover the door closed. Kicking it open, I saw Pandak sharing her mat with Agni-pan. Enraged, Agni-pan demanded to know why I had surprised them. As quietly as I could, I told him I had not come to find him in bed with my wife. I did not want to draw the attention of the people at the poncion. If they came, embarrassment to Pandak and Agni-pan would have been unavoidable.

Though Agni-pan wanted to leave, Pandak urged him to remain with us for the night. Strangely, I was relieved. This would serve as a justification for me to separate from Pandak, so I encouraged him also. I lay down in another corner to indicate I was going to leave them alone. I truly was physically tired. When I woke the next morning, the sun was well up and there was no sign of Agni-pan. Pandak was still sleeping.

Coming out of the hut, I saw Agni-pan talking with his father on Ang-gin's fantao. When Ang-gin joined them, I told him I was leaving his daughter that same day. I reminded him she had gained the claim on me that she had wanted. It was evident this was her only interest in marrying me; hence, it was pointless for me to live with her any longer. I told Agni-pan his family still owed me an otang kahuri, which brought a grimace from him. Malay-ay asked if I had said "otang kahuri" or "otang pangayofan." Otang pangayofan means an obligation for a generous deed, and otang kahuri means a debt for a dishonorable act. I told Malay-ay his son knew which I meant. I then left them.

Pandak asked where I was going when she saw me packing my bayong. I bluntly told her she had achieved her aim, so I was leaving. Our marriage was ended.

19 My Life in Siangi Ends

Although I might be the prodigal son returning to my foster-father in repentance, Agaw's response was not that of the father in the story the Omang Ugalis told. My many returns after foolish ventures had worn out his forgiving spirit. Agaw treated me as a lost soul. He did not even mention my latest escapade, though he must have heard of it, since the scandal was known throughout Siangi.

One day Yonay had an unexpected visit from her aunt, Yam-nay, who had come all the way from the western part of Mindoro with her son and grandson, because of a rumor that there were bountiful harvests in Siangi. After Yonay explained that Siangi harvests had been sparse too, she appealed to Lando, who might know where there was a good harvest.

The only possible harvest Lando knew of was a rice crop in Ayofay. I blurted out that I knew the way to Ayofay. Before I could say another word, Yonay thanked me for offering to guide her aunt there. I was relieved that I was again considered a son who could be expected to help in family duties.

We left early the next morning. During our long journey, Yam-nay told many stories about her experiences in curing people while traveling around Siangi. She was famous for her cures. She was one of the very few women fangamlangs. I was curious about some of her difficult cases, but instead of answering my many questions, she distracted me with folk legends, such as the story of a prince named Falyos, who had defeated three kings, each of whom had eight eyes. Falyos married the beautiful princess Daga and decreed himself king. He forbade all weapons of war. He promised our people years and years of peace if they would follow his rules. King Falyos and Queen Daga, in appreciation of the loyalty of a particular dog and cat, ordered all cats and dogs to be loved, protected, and finally buried with respect. We still follow this custom. By another special decree, wild doves could not be hunted or eaten. That law, too, is still in effect.

The owner of the rice crop—a man named Ang-gin—and his wife were delighted to see us. Ang-gin recognized Aunt Yam-nay immediately, and remembered me as having married Li-maynan, who was well known in that area. He was honored that we had traveled so far to work his harvest.

That first evening a young couple who were neighbors visited us. They made special friendly approaches to me. I learned they also planned to work the harvest. The first night of the harvest they invited me to sleep in their home. I heard them discussing me while I pretended to be sleeping. Although they had been married three years they had not yet

123

had a child. The wife had given birth in a previous marriage, so they wanted me to sleep with her.

Among the Buhids of Siangi it is a common practice, though never openly admitted, for a sterile husband, who wants children, to encourage his wife to have sex with another man. It is agreed that the man the husband selects will be charged with alienation, and will pay the normal fine for his offense. After the woman is pregnant the man is given back the fine. I slept with the man's wife that night. In the morning we joined the group who were going to Akling to work in the harvest of a man named Naay.

A poncion was given by Ganit, a neighbor, on the first evening of the Akling harvest. I met Amit there with Naay's daughter, Alot. Amit mentioned that I had been her first husband, and quickly added that we had been separated for a long time. When Alot came over to borrow tobacco that evening, I matted down with her for the night.

We saw Alot's parents the next day, and they consented to our marriage after only a few questions to me. We went through the usual mat and blanket ceremony, and I gave Naay one arm's length of panaongens as my dowry.

My marriage to Alot ended with the harvest on her father's kaingin four days later. She was insufferably domineering, and reminded me too much of Lando's former wife. On the last day of the harvest Alot and I agreed to separate.

As we traveled back to Siangi Aunt Yam-nay advised me on my morals. She told me to marry only that girl I truly loved, and she asked me to make a distinction between love and lust. She was so sincere, I promised her I would try very hard to remember and follow her instructions.

Chief Agaw was reserved toward me when we got back to his home; in fact, he seemed to ignore me entirely. I learned from Lando that Agaw's family had been invited to a two-night poncion being given by Balitang, the village guardian, before his harvest. I attended the first night with Rahoyan, Lando, and Lohena.

During the poncion a boiling-water test was to be given to two men accused of stealing a chicken. The test would prove which of them was lying about his part in the crime.

Way-day had accused Lupoy of stealing the chicken. Lupoy

admitted his guilt, but named Ren-nay as his accomplice. Ren-nay, however, said he was innocent. Ren-nay and Lupoy agreed to take the test. To do this they each had to pick a stone out of a pot of boiling water. The one whose hand was not scalded would be innocent.

In a flash, Lupoy withdrew the stone and threw it back into the pot again. Ren-nay did the same. Lupoy's hand had no injury, while Ren-nay's hand was swollen and red. Each of them was fined for stealing the chicken, and Ren-nay was given an additional fine for lying.

Another test used to determine which of two people is lying is the test by the chicken's beak. The accuser sits on the ground across from the person he claims is lying. The two are eight feet apart. A judge, after reciting the proper instructions, slits the throat of a chicken and places the bird between the two antagonists. It is believed that at the moment of death the chicken will point its beak at the liar. The person thus pointed out is fined. If the chicken points at neither, they are both innocent.

The poncion was just starting when I met a beautiful girl who invited me to eat with her and some friends. We joined her four girl friends, and because none of them introduced themselves, I remained silent and enjoyed the excellent food. When we finished eating we all separated, and I wandered off without learning the girl's name. Later in the evening she invited me to sleep in her house that night. When I accepted she took me to a big house full of people, told me to find a place to sleep, and vanished again.

In the morning, except for a few children, I was the only one in the house. The poncion was still going. I discovered that my mysterious hostess was Yaoy, Balitang's daughter. That day Yaoy saw that I was served a fine midday meal and supper. The deep feeling within me that Yaoy excited seemed to fit the definition of love that Yam-nay had given me. She had offered me rest and food, but had not flirted with me.

On the first day of the harvest in her father's kaingin, Yaoy received the rice turned in by each harvester. When I gave her what I had picked, so it could be divided into two shares, Yaoy put all of it back into my bayong. I asked her why she did not deduct her father's share, but she did not answer. It was obvious that the other young men were not pleased. Their rivalry was understandable, for Yaoy was the prettiest girl in Siangi.

The next day, when Yaoy again refused to deduct her father's share from the rice I had picked, I challenged her about being so careless with her father's interest in the harvest. She explained that the kaingin I was working belonged to her and not to her father. I explained, apologetically, that I had been threatened by the other boys because of her special consideration. She was aware of the situation. She also knew all about my marriage to Alot, because her husband, Aynay, had separated from her to marry Alot shortly after Alot and I separated. Yaoy invited me to sleep in her hut on her kaingin. That night we consummated our marriage. I was certain I now understood the true meaning of love, and I was equally certain I wanted Yaoy to be my lifetime partner.

We adjusted quickly to married life, planning to expand our kaingin, preparing to plant the next crop of corn, and gathering materials to repair our hut. Returning from the forest one afternoon, I suffered a painful headache, but did not complain to Yaoy since I believed it would pass. By nightfall I had fever and severe diarrhea. Yaoy was a perfect nurse, putting wet cloths on my head to get the fever down, and preparing barks and herbs to my directions. Still my fever continued to rise and I was delirious the whole night. Hearing Yaoy describe my symptoms, her father decided I had chicken pox. Balitang had learned there was an epidemic nearby.

For the next three days, sores covered my entire body and made it painful to lie down. Yaoy disregarded my warnings to stay away from me and continued to nurse me. When the sores subsided, I was tormented by itching so agonizing that even with Yaoy and me both scratching I could not get relief. When I began to recover my strength we went on short walks together. My love for Yaoy intensified.

A few days after my recovery, Agaw sent me a message by a friend to come to him. After I told Yaoy, I took her to her father's. I wanted her to stay with him until I returned.

Balitang must have had some inkling of what Agaw wanted because he assured me that if Agaw disapproved of my marriage to his daughter I was still welcome to return. I promised each of them I would be back regardless of Agaw.

Emian, Severino Luna, and Bag-etan in Siangi, January 1971.

Agaw was furious. I had never seen him so angry with me as at that meeting. I answered all his questions about my marriage. Agaw ordered me either to cut my ties with Yaoy or prepare to cut my ties to his family under the provisions of a formal fandayohan hiano. I was too shocked to give an immediate reply to his ultimatum.

Under a fandayohan hiano a person formally severs his ties to his family. He must pay his parents an estimated cost for his care from the day he was born to the moment of the severance. The child stops being claimed or recognized by the parents as their child, and the child no longer considers the parents as his or even as relatives. Once imposed, the fandayohan hiano is irrevocable.

127

Severino Luna with group of Mangyans.

For a man of Agaw's fairness to adopt such an attitude meant there must be substantial reason. It was widely known that Agaw and Yonay had taken me in and accepted me as a son. If I now asked for a fandayohan hiano, I would be called an ingrate. The rebuffs Yaoy and I would encounter would have a bad effect on our marriage. My deep love for Yaoy had to be sacrificed. I could not subject her to such an ordeal. I made the decision to separate from Yaoy, and Agaw agreed that I must be the one to tell her.

My swollen and reddened eyes told Yaoy the sad news. When I tried to explain, I started to cry. She did not press the subject, hoping the crisis would pass. I thought about going away while Yaoy was sleeping and leaving the bad news in a message, but Yaoy deserved more consideration than that. I told her, and left immediately afterward.

Agaw resented Yaoy's father because he had paid Eg-hay's fine during the confrontation over the death of Agaw's son Baban. Had Balitang not paid Eg-hay's fine Agaw could have punished Eg-hay for killing his son.

128

Severino Luna with Bag-etan, 1971.

Preserving old enmities often brings injustice to innocent persons. While Agaw's desire for revenge against Balitang may have been justified, his objection to my marrying Balitang's daughter harmed me more than it did Balitang. Try as I might, I could not stop grieving for Yaoy.

The news that the Major was soon coming back to his plantation fired my hopes of going with him to Manila, where I could forget. In the next weeks, which dragged endlessly, I did nothing but attend poncions and have short-lived affairs.

The night we saw the fireworks signal the Major's arrival, Agaw decided we should all make the pilgrimage to visit the Major. The next morning, as we traveled, I asked Agaw to talk to the Major about taking me to Manila, and the Chief was

Bag-etan at seventeen.

quite receptive. I learned Agaw had been to Manila himself. He warned me to stay ever alert to the endless iron cars and trucks that perpetually move like great foraging ants and run over anyone who dares get in their way.

A large meal was served to all of us who visited the Major that afternoon, during which he told thrilling tales about his travels to strange and distant places. When we were finally alone with him, I heard Chief Agaw mention my name. The Major asked a Mr. Arroyo to talk to me. Mr. Arroyo asked me a few questions without giving me any clue as to whether I could count on going to Manila. After that Mr. Arroyo and he talked, and the Major told us he would be back in four days. He told Agaw to bring me to his farm then, ready to travel. I was so happy, I embraced the Major and kissed him. He seemed surprised and pleased.

I went to the Major's farm a day early to find out what time he wanted me to be there, and he urged me to stay for the night, so we could get an early start. I met Simeona, a young Logtanon girl, who was also going to Manila with the Major for the first time. Both of us were excited. Simeona and I were taken for a long walk to a bus stop, and Mr. Arroyo took us on the bus to a town where he bought us clothing.

The next day, as we boarded the bus that would take us on the first part of our trip, I headed for the baggage compartment where the Buhids always must ride, but the Major had me sit beside him in the very front seats. Only then did I realize I was no longer wearing only a G-string. When we reached the seaport town of Bongabon, the bus left us at the pier. There we were to take a ferry across to the city of Batangas on the main island of Luzon.

I did not look forward to the boat ride, recalling the many songs the elders sing about disasters of the "houses that float on the water." After we had survived several safe hours, I began to enjoy being on a boat. I was fascinated by the stairs that connected to another floor above the one we stood on. The boat was much larger than our houses in the forest, and I was amazed at the number of people. The water was so calm, I could not stay fearful. I fell in love with the reflections the stars made on the sea.

20 A New Jungle of Noises, Lights, Roads, Buses, Accidents, Clinics

In Batangas we boarded a large bus to take us to Manila. The driver was in such a hurry to reach the city, I thought evil spirits were chasing him. When another bus passed us, our driver started to race after it. He became alarmingly reckless, trying to pass the other bus. The Major and other passengers started shouting at him to slow down, but before he could, he lost whatever control he had. The bus slid into a canal and

131

plowed a deep furrow in the road, ending with a loud crash.

In the darkness after our crash landing, I could hear the groans and cries of women and children. The Major asked Mr. Arroyo if he was all right. After his response, the Major yelled my name, and I assured him I was not injured. When he shouted for Simeona there was no reply. I heard the Major tell Mr. Arroyo his back and legs hurt him. Anxiously he repeated his shouts for Simeona.

Someone struck a match, but another person immediately put it out, screaming there were too many gas fumes, so we were back in total darkness with the anguished cries of the injured. I wondered if poor Simeona was lying dead somewhere in the bus. The songs the old people sing about the dangers of boat travel kept surging through my head. The forest had no danger like a man with a motor on a paved street racing another driver to prove he could go faster. Perhaps the elders would change their songs about boats if they ever learned about buses.

The three of us yelled for Simeona while we searched for her through the mess of overturned seats and bodies. Rays of light from the same kind of hand-lights Rausig had used suddenly appeared. The passengers inside the bus, seeing that help had come, began to recover from the shock of the accident and to climb out of the wreckage. The door was forced open so people could escape through it.

Mr. Arroyo and I urged the Major to get out of the bus, but he insisted on searching for Simeona. Then I saw her standing outside. The Major and Mr. Arroyo were both greatly relieved.

The conductor recognized Mr. Arroyo and me as former passengers, so we were allowed to go back in to get our baggage. He was protecting the property on the bus from possible looters. Simeona told us she could not remember how she got outside. After hearing the noise of the crash, she found herself lying on the ground.

We were taken to a clinic in a police jeep for treatment of the Major's injuries and the minor ones suffered by the three of us. The nurse painted Simeona and me with red medicine, but the Logtanon fangamlang had the Major taken into a room, where they closed the door to take pictures to find out how seriously he was damaged. It was a mystery to me for a long time how a camera could take a picture of a person's insides. It was decided, after studying the picture, that the Major could travel to his home in Manila to see another fangamlang.

We were put on another bus, and the Major was soon fast asleep. When I asked how the Major could sleep with the pains he had, Mr. Arroyo explained that the Logtanons had a pill which could make you sleep under any conditions. Mr. Arroyo pointed out to Simeona and me the many sights we passed. I noticed with concern that as we got closer to Manila the number of motor vehicles on the road increased. When we entered a long straight road, Mr. Arroyo said the bus driver had to pay money to travel on it. The bus started going so fast I could hardly catch my breath. I begged Mr. Arroyo to get the driver to slow down, since I was sure we would have another accident, but he refused, claiming the driver was going the Logtanons' normal speed. As I saw it, the driver paid money so that he could drive fast enough to make sure he had an accident. When I saw stone houses which reached so high as to almost go through the sky, I could not imagine what sort of people would live there. They must live in constant fear of falling out.

At the first stop the bus made, the Major woke up, but he was still feeling pain in his back and legs. After a few more stops, we got off and into a small car, which the Major called a taxi. The taxi driver tried just as hard as the bus driver to get us into an accident. I sat in the back with the Major, and he pointed out many interesting things to me. The incredible number of speeding vehicles, the loud noises, and the frantic activity of city streets made me dizzy. We stopped at a store where the Major's wife came out to greet us, and the Major introduced each of us.

The Major's wife arrived at their house a short time after we did, and I told her that her husband had gone to lie down. To my amazement, she picked up from a table something which looked like a black bone, and after doing something with the black part that was still on the table, started talking to somebody, but I could not see who it was. No one else was in the room. After she finished talking to the black thing, she put it back and started talking to me.

Before going to sleep that night, I reflected for a long time on the many strange and wonderful things I had seen in Manila that first day.

Glossary of Buhid Words

Abul. Short blouse worn by girls

Afoyo. Hammock

Aswang. Night spirit that enters house as a bat, changes into upper half of human body, and sucks blood

Baboy gayat. Evil spirit that roams at night

Baboy talon. Wild pig

Badil. Shotgun

Baglaw. Small slimy fish

Bahay bahayan. Tiny hut to hold personal belongings of newly deceased person

Baksonan. Test to determine if a sick person is ready to eat meat

Balitangan taw. One who acts as a judge

Baruka. Woven breast band worn by girls

Bayong. Woven pouch bag

Binhaven. Large circle on ground for rice seedlings

Bitlag. Bamboo tube inscribed with messages or songs

Bodbodan. Community planting

Bok sirang. Noon; sun at zenith

Buri. Palm fiber woven into sleeping mats

Camote. Wild sweet potato

Cogon. Marsh grass used in bundles for roofs and siding of huts

Dalidan. Trunk of large tree which is beaten to send messages of alarm

Dangao. Measurement from stretched thumb to tip of fifth finger

Daniws. Exorcisms; chants intoned by healers

Depa. Measurement from left shoulder, across back, to tip of middle finger of right hand

Duak. Two

Duhat. A tree with medicinal roots

Edick. Broad leaves from a tree, woven into a rain hood-cape

Embasan mama. A cud of chewing tobacco

Faagap. A warning signal set near an animal trap

Fafituwan Fag Sirang Kati Kanatoy. Seventh day after death

Fagablang. Evil spirit which causes human sickness

Falafay. Beehive

Famahowayon. A nap; a rest period

Familibana. Consolation prize paid to losing suitor by winner

Familibang hasadi hasadi. Act of breaking up a courtship

Famogad. Symbol of good luck in hunting, a root tied to a spear

Famuayong. Local postmaster

Fana fofo. A person who acts as lawyer in defense

Fandia surat. Message carrier

Fanduat surat. Message censor

Fangabaya. An investigation of wrongdoing

Fangamlang. Medicine man; healer

Faniningonan. Victory in winning a girl from many suitors

Fanlahiyans. Prayer chanters at funerals

Fanlalatoy. Cannibal

Fanligao baboy. Special messengers who find white chickens and pigs for ceremonial use

Fan-ngagawan. Victory in winning a girl from one suitor

Fanoyaw. Large fighter monkey

Fantao. Balcony entrance to a hut

Farayfayon. Legendary Muslim who invaded Siangi, killed and ate women

Fasongsongan. Roofed shelter pitched in forest as rain shield

Fatahoyan. Parental consent to marriage of a daughter

Fumisilague. Act of deception; giving a suitor false hope

Gabi. Root vegetable

Gal hag. Cutting and piling branches in clearing a kaingin

Gamas. Cutting shrubs and undergrowth

Gubang wan. Cutting small trees

Habag. Tree feared by snakes; used by travelers for shelter

Halayan. Shrimp with long claws and big heads

Heling. Hollowed bamboo tube about five feet long, used for carrying water

Hinoyo. Dowry offered to father of prospective bride

Hiyan guragon. Local magistrate who can impose fines

Kaingin. Clearing in the forest prepared for planting crops

Labang bayan. An evil spirit that turns into a giant cannibal at night

Litlit. Betelnut leaves

Llagan. Good spirit which cures human sickness

Logtanon. Any person from outside a specific settlement

Magdadaniw. A person who can communicate with both good and evil spirits

Maman-tohoyan. A suitor

Man fatahoyan. Formal visit by suitor to request parents' permission to marry their daughter

Manlaby. Last step in preparing a kaingin, burning dried trees and shrubs

Mascada. Chewing tobacco

Mianit kalimbaba. About midafternoon, 3 P.M.

Mianit mashohod mita. Midmorning, about 10 A.M., sun at 45 degrees

Nanay. Mother

Napnoan sa gamat. About 2 P.M.

Oliso. A loud cry announcing the moment of death

Omang Ugali. Christian religion

Otang kahuri. A debt for a dishonorable act

Otang pangayofan. An obligation in return for a generous deed

Panaongens. Strings of bright multicolored beads used as payment of fines

Pangati. Wild chicken trap

Pasaruk luban gamat. Hand ritual in greeting

Poncion. Party, feast

Rokiawan. Distance a human shout can be heard

Rorum. An old dull bead

Saba. Green bananas

Sagaba. Flat wickerwork tray for food or for winnowing rice

Sahing. A torch soaked in tree sap

Salabay. Necklace of twigs; omen of good hunting

Sanbong. A piece of iron with a wooden handle

Santik magurang. Pieces of flint for friction lighting

Sayogubang sayong tipco. Next to last step in preparing a clearing, cutting down large trees

Sindogo. Blood brother, kinsman

Tagadia. Messenger

Tagadia fanganons. A relief worker

Tagadia taga-ahon. An arresting officer

Tamolo. An inscriber

Tatay. Father

Taya. A cup; half a coconut shell

Tuway. A clam shell